G000270385

BRITAIN'S PARANORMAL FORESTS

ABOUT THE AUTHOR

DR PETER A. McCUE is a retired clinical psychologist who lives in Scotland. His interest in anomalous phenomena goes back decades, and he has personally investigated many cases, as well as writing numerous articles on paranormal and UFO matters, and being interviewed for radio, internet and television. *Britain's Paranormal Forests* is the much-anticipated follow-up to *Paranormal Encounters on Britain's Roads: Phantom Figures, UFOs and Missing Time* (The History Press, 2018).

BRITAIN'S PARANORMAL FORESTS

ENCOUNTERS IN THE WOODS

PETER A. McCUE

First published 2019

The History Press
97 St George's Place, Cheltenham,
Gloucestershire, GL50 3QB
www.thehistorypress.co.uk

© Peter McCue, 2019

The right of Peter McCue to be identified as the Author
of this work has been asserted in accordance with the
Copyright, Designs and Patents Act 1988.

All rights reserved. No part of this book may be reprinted
or reproduced or utilised in any form or by any electronic,
mechanical or other means, now known or hereafter invented,
including photocopying and recording, or in any information
storage or retrieval system, without the permission in writing
from the Publishers.

British Library Cataloguing in Publication Data.
A catalogue record for this book is available from the British Library.

ISBN 978 0 7509 9133 9

Typesetting and origination by The History Press
Printed and bound in Great Britain by TJ International Ltd

MIX
Paper from
responsible sources
FSC
www.fsc.org
FSC® C013056

CONTENTS

ACKNOWLEDGEMENTS

I should like to thank Rob Gandy for kindly writing the Foreword to this book, as well as for other assistance. I'm very grateful to my friend David T. Muir for his help with proofreading. I'm also appreciative of the people who've given me accounts of their strange experiences. My thanks go to Justin Williams for providing information and source material for Chapter 2, and to the British Geological Survey for information relevant to Chapter 3. I'm grateful to the Rev. Johanna Clare and W. John Hoyland for the photographs included in Chapter 4; and I'd like to thank Barbara Fennell for providing material for that chapter. Regarding Chapter 7, I'm grateful to Ron Halliday, for showing me the site of Robert Taylor's strange encounter near Livingston, Scotland, and to Nigel Watson, for sending me an article that he'd written on the case. I'd like to thank Steve Wills, for information that he sent me pertaining to a case mentioned in Chapter 9. Finally, I should like to thank an informant, who has requested anonymity, for information included in Chapter 2.

FOREWORD

'If you go down in the woods today, You're sure of a big surprise …' according to the song by Henry Hall & His Orchestra back in 1932. And as you will read in this book, many people have had *very* big surprises when they have been in Britain's woods, and they were not as pleasant as coming across a group of teddy bears having a picnic. No, some were puzzling, some were scary, and some were downright nasty.

Woods and forests represent around 13 per cent of the total land area in the UK, with the greatest concentrations in Wales and Scotland. They have always been places of mystery, sanctuary and enchantment, and are both enticing and unsettling at the same time. Woods and forests form the backdrop for many of the fairy stories that we are told as children, and are the explicit locations of adventurers such as Robin Hood. So it is arguable that we are primed from an early age to be alert to things that might only be seen out of the corner of one eye, when we travel their leafy or pine-scattered paths. But it is at night that woods and forests become particularly forbidding, with absolute darkness and silence punctuated by the cries of foxes, the screeches of owls and the muffled sounds of things unseen moving close by. Any inexplicable lights will demand our attention.

In his previous book *Paranormal Encounters on Britain's Roads*, Peter McCue examined a wide range of weird phenomena and experiences, and allocated them according to their type, rather than their location. But in this book he focuses on one particular type of location – woodland – and examines a number of 'classic' cases, and others that might be less well known. These feature stories about strange lights and sounds, UFOs, ghosts and black magic. They also encompass diverse creatures such as Alien Big Cats, Werewolves, Bigfoot and Owlman!

Many authors focus on one location or one phenomenon, but Peter takes the admirable stance that maybe *all* apparitions and otherworldly creatures that people experience in woods, on roads, or wherever, are part of the same phenomenon; it's just that it can manifest in a kaleidoscope of different ways. This leads him to explore how it might be that this is the case, using examples from across the world to illustrate how varying phenomena have sometimes come together in one place.

Where Peter scores highly, in my opinion, is that he presents material from the available sources (sometimes augmented by his own field research) in an open-minded and conversational way. His evaluations reflect his clinical background, and that he is a cautious believer in the reality of the phenomena. As a good fortean, he is convinced that strange things happen, but he is by no means certain *how* and *why* they occur. Inevitably there are inconsistencies between some of the testimonies, and therefore Peter sets things out for you as the reader so that you can consider the quality and consistency of events, and evaluate potential causes and explanations yourself. Naturally, he adds his own comments about their veracity, and proffers potential explanations, sometimes with a touch of his wry humour. He also provides good notes and a bibliography so that you, as the reader, can follow up on any of the cases with ease. His thorough approach contrasts with that of some others who write about such experiences as though they are simply telling (their preferred version of) a story, with no validation of the evidence and no mention of the fact that there might be several, conflicting sources; the reader is expected to believe what is written because it is there in black and white in front of their eyes.

Of course, variations in witnesses' accounts do not necessarily mean that they were mistaken or are lying. Sceptics will always use this to dismiss unusual or paranormal experiences. But if you go to a criminal court, you will see that witnesses to a given incident will invariably provide differing and often conflicting testimonies whilst on oath. Such variation is not used to say that the incident did not take place; it is seen as part of the fact that witnesses can see and interpret things differently, for whatever reason.

As Charles Fort realised, science often dismisses phenomena that do not fit with the existing scientific paradigm. This does not mean that the phenomena are not real; it might just be that science has not yet caught up with the phenomena. And as science advances, then such phenomena may well become accepted, as was the case with meteors and the giant squid. But if the details of such phenomena are rejected out of hand and not recorded, then how is science to analyse relevant data?

So do Bigfoot and his fellow incredible creatures actually exist? Peter refers to the possibilities of some of them being associated with UFOs or being of an 'inter-dimensional' origin.

But I would like to think that it's simply a case of the final words of *The Teddy Bears' Picnic*, which state: 'Beneath the trees where nobody sees, they'll hide …'

Rob Gandy

Dr Rob Gandy is a Visiting Professor at Liverpool Business School, Liverpool John Moore's University, and a regular contributor to the magazine *Fortean Times*.

PREFACE

This book examines reports of people having strange experiences in woodland areas of Great Britain. The focus on woodland is very personal: I've always felt that there's something romantic and enchanting about woods and forests, particularly broadleaf woodland. Sadly, with population growth and 'development', Britain has lost much of its natural woodland over the years, and threats continue. So far as paranormal and UFO events are concerned, I have no grounds for claiming that woods and forests attract a disproportionate amount of such activity, although it wouldn't entirely surprise me if that turned out to be the case. However, there certainly are numerous reports on record of people having anomalous experiences in our woods and forests, and many instances are discussed below.

I regard myself as a cautious believer in the reality of paranormal phenomena, but I don't hold fast to any particular theory. In other words, I'm convinced that strange things happen, but I'm by no means certain *how* and *why* they occur.

I've referenced sources within the main text or in the endnotes for each chapter. In citing books in the endnotes, I've given just the main title and omitted the year of publication and details of the publisher. But this information is provided in the Bibliography. By the time this book is published, some of the cited internet items may no longer be accessible via the addresses given. But by using a search engine such as Google it may be possible to find them elsewhere on the internet.

Except where indicated, I've used real names in referring to witnesses with whom I've had personal contact. With regard to the names cited by other authors, the situation isn't so clear, since (regrettably, in my view) writers don't always say when they're using pseudonyms. But where I'm aware that pseudonyms have been used, I've indicated that. I haven't changed any place names, and hopefully that's also the case with the places mentioned by the authors I cite.

In quoting people, I've occasionally edited the material very slightly for presentational purposes, but I haven't changed the substantive content. In Chapter 6, I've cited a book by Lee Brickley, which was published with some slight errors in its main title: *UFOS Werewolves & The Pig-Man*. In referencing the book, I've corrected the errors, rendering the title as *UFOs, Werewolves & the Pig-Man*. Similarly, in referencing Volume 2 of Malcolm Robinson's *UFO Case Files of Scotland*, I've edited the subtitle, to remove an error, and to make it stylistically consistent with the subtitle of the first volume.

The majority of the photographs appearing in this book were taken by me. In the two instances where that wasn't the case, I've included the name of the photographer (W.J. Hoyland) in the captions.

At points, I mention distances between places. These should be understood as straight line ('as the crow flies') distances, not road-travel distances.

Being somewhat old-fashioned, I generally think in terms of Imperial measures (e.g. miles, feet and inches) rather than their metric equivalents. Accordingly, I've used these traditional measures. But where I've cited authors who've used the metric system, I've largely given the measures in the form that they've reported them. However, in respect of hills, I've given heights in both metres and feet.

Regarding the index, I haven't included the names of all the witnesses mentioned throughout the book, since some of the cases are little known and, in many instances, the people referred to may have been given pseudonyms.

1

INTRODUCTION

With only 13 per cent of tree cover, the UK is one of the least wooded parts of Europe. Northern Ireland rates particularly low on tree cover, and the Republic of Ireland is also relatively devoid of woodland.[1] However, in looking at reports of paranormal activity associated with woodland, I'll focus on mainland Britain rather than on the British Isles as a whole.

Of course, our woodland cover was much more extensive in past centuries. Population growth and industrialisation have taken a heavy toll. Sadly, we have very little ancient woodland left. Our largest forests are now of the planted, coniferous type, and they tend to be a rather sterile environment for wildlife.

There's constant pressure on our woodland, and the country-side more generally, from 'development' projects of one sort or another. The developers and their political backers claim that a balance needs to be struck between conservation and the demand for houses, roads, railway lines and so on. Unfortunately, though, it always seems to be the natural environment that loses out. For example, we never seem to hear of developed land being returned to Mother Nature!

This book consists of three main parts: a series of detailed case studies (Chapters 2–8), a penultimate chapter that looks, more briefly, at a wide range of reports from around Britain, and then a concluding chapter, which – among other things – cites cases of interest from overseas.

A NOTE ON TERMINOLOGY

THE EXPRESSION 'UFO'

Many of the cases mentioned in this book involved strange lights or UFOs. 'UFO' stands for *unidentified flying object* and is widely applied to all sorts of unknown or anomalous aerial phenomena, ranging from sightings of structured craft to small balls of light.[2] In theory, it's possible to distinguish between anomalous aerial lights and aerial objects that seem to be structured craft. The latter might be more correctly described as UFOs than the former. However, even lights without an identifiable structure sometimes act as if they were under intelligent control. Furthermore, if a witness is unable to discern any structure within, or behind, aerial lights, it doesn't necessarily mean that there is none. Therefore, I shan't try to draw a hard and fast distinction between 'lights' and 'UFOs'.

A problem with the term 'UFO' is that it's not always clear whether *objects* as such are responsible for the sightings. Indeed, many UFO experiences may be hallucinatory experiences, albeit of a paranormal nature – see below. Another problem is that some people automatically equate UFOs with alien spaceships, although that's just one of many possible interpretations. Objects on the ground that could be construed as landed aerial craft of unidentified origin are also referred to as

UFOs. It's also worth noting that UFOs are sometimes seen to enter, or emerge from, the sea or other bodies of water, and that mysterious underwater objects have reportedly been detected by equipment.

I'll refer to the study of UFOs as *ufology*, and to people who pursue this interest as *ufologists*, irrespective of how they interpret the reported phenomena. On investigation, many UFOs lose their unidentified status. For example, mysterious lights in the sky might turn out to be space debris burning up on re-entry to the atmosphere, or balloons, bright planets, Chinese lanterns, or other natural or man-made objects.

HALLUCINATIONS

Hallucinations are believed-in perceptual experiences occurring in the absence of an objectively real stimulus. For example, if I see a black dog that's not physically present and which can't be detected with recording equipment, my experience might be described as hallucinatory. A distinction can be made between *true hallucinations* and *pseudo-hallucinations*. A true hallucination is when the witness believes that his or her false perception is objectively real. But if the percipient knows that what's being experienced is subjective, it can be described as a pseudo-hallucination. Imagine, for instance, that you're under the influence of LSD and that you notice that the cushions on your sofa are 'breathing'. If you realise that your experience is subjective – that the cushions aren't really breathing – your experience could be classed as a pseudo-hallucination.

Witnesses to paranormal events might take offence if it's suggested that their experiences were hallucinatory. They might infer that their mental stability is being questioned and that the paranormal nature of their experiences is being denied. However, it may be that some experiences are both hallucinatory *and* paranormal. For example, if witnesses recurrently see an apparition in a haunted house over a long period of time, this would suggest that something paranormal is going on, irrespective of whether the appearances are hallucinatory.

A popular assumption is that if two or more people simultaneously experience the same thing (seeing a ghost, for instance), that proves that it isn't hallucinatory. However, if we accept that paranormal experiences occur, there could well be *collective hallucinations* of a paranormal nature. In practice, though, it's often hard to know whether anomalous experiences are hallucinatory or have an objective basis.

Haunt phenomena often leave no physical trace, which could mean that they're hallucinatory. Take, for example, a case that was drawn to my attention in 1999. It involved industrial premises in the east of Scotland. One of my informants was Isobel (pseudonym), who'd worked there as a cleaner. At one point, she and a fellow worker heard something being dragged across the floor of an office above them. But when she went upstairs and looked into the room, she saw nothing out of place.[3] In a similar vein, the late Andrew MacKenzie reported a London-based case in which a witness, in her bedroom, heard noises downstairs, including bangs and crashes. When she went downstairs in the morning, she was surprised to find nothing out of place. But whether or not the sounds were hallucinatory, there also appeared to be some physical effects (unless we're to assume that they, too, were hallucinatory). For example, the aforementioned witness entered a room to find that a box containing some beads had disappeared. She left the room but found the box back in position when she returned five minutes later. And her father witnessed an incident in which five bedroom doors banged shut, one after another.[4]

THE 'ALIEN ABDUCTION' PHENOMENON

Because it's a subject that crops up in some of the following chapters, I'll say a few introductory words about the 'alien abduction' phenomenon.

After UFO sightings, particularly 'close encounters', witnesses are sometimes unable to account for passages of time. They might be haunted by vague feelings, flashbacks and partial recollections; and they might discover marks, scars or apparent 'implants' that they hadn't previously noticed. Over time, or with the aid of the controversial technique of hypnotic regression, they might recall abduction scenarios involving otherworldly entities. Accounts often feature medical examinations and reproductive procedures, and it's been suggested that non-humans are systematically creating human-alien hybrids and using female abductees as incubators, perhaps as part of a programme aimed at taking over our planet.[5] At any rate, irrespective of whether the reported abductions are physically real or are paranormal, trickster-imposed experiences with a hallucinatory element, they're usually distressing for the people involved. For many victims, the experiences are recurrent. Different generations within a family might be targeted. Thus, a woman with a history of distressing abduction experiences might be dismayed to learn that her daughter is going through a similar ordeal.

A GEOGRAPHICAL NOTE

Some of the cases discussed in this book are from the West Midlands region of England. However, the term 'West Midlands' is ambiguous, because it's also applies to a metropolitan county and city region within the broader West Midlands region.

KEEPING SAFE IN THE WOODS

Britain's woods and forests are comparatively small. For visitors, this obviously reduces the likelihood of getting lost in them, although it's always worth having a decent map and taking a compass. However, it may be virtually impossible to follow a straight compass line through densely spaced trees in commercial woodland. And with fresh planting and the bulldozing of new tracks, maps of artificially forested areas can soon become out of date.

It's sensible to take plenty of fluid and sufficient warm clothing on excursions into the wild. In the event of an accident, it's helpful to have a first-aid kit, a torch and a fully charged mobile phone. Before venturing into a relatively remote area, particularly in winter, it's advisable to inform a friend or relative of one's intended route and expected time of return.

On the whole, the animals inhabiting Britain's woods and forests pose few threats to human visitors. However, driving at speed through wooded areas puts motorists at risk of colliding with animals crossing roads, particularly deer. In Hampshire's New Forest, motorists might also encounter ponies on the minor roads. If woods or forests are approached via pastures containing cattle, walkers should be careful not to alarm them. For example, it's wise to avoid walking between cows and their calves.

Three types of snake are native to Britain. The smooth snake, which is non-venomous, is confined to heathland in the far south of England. The grass snake, which can be found in England and Wales, is fond of wetland habitats, but it can also be found in dry grasslands and in gardens, especially if there's a pond nearby. Like the smooth snake, it's non-venomous. The adder is more widely distributed throughout Britain. Although venomous, it's by nature a shy creature and is much more inclined to avoid humans than bite them, unless it's picked up or trodden on. Like all snakes, adders are deaf, but sensitive to vibrations. Their bites are rarely fatal, but it's worth seeking medical advice if one is bitten.

Wild boar were once a native woodland species in Britain, but were hunted to extinction in the Middle Ages. In the 1980s, boar farming became prevalent, and it's believed that many boar escaped, or were illegally released into the wild. There are now established breeding populations in places such as the Weald (an area between the North and South Downs in south-east England) and the Forest of Dean. Given that wild boar are mainly nocturnal, the chances of walkers encountering them are slim. They're of a shy disposition and will usually flee if they detect people. But like many other animals, they may become aggressive if they feel under threat. That's especially so, of course, in respect of females with their young. It's recommended that dogs be kept on a lead in woods inhabited by wild boar. If a walker encounters one, it's advisable for him or her to retreat slowly in the opposite direction.

Ticks are small, blood-sucking, spider-like insects. They prey mainly on animals such as deer and sheep, but they aren't averse to targeting humans. I can speak personally on this, because there've been times when I've found ticks on my body after hillwalking trips or woodland excursions. On one occasion, I found a live tick on me *five days* after a hillwalking trip – they seem resistant to baths and showers, and they can be very hard to spot! They're a health risk, because some of them carry pathogens, such as *Borrelia burgdorferi* bacteria, which cause Lyme disease.[6] Untreated, this is a serious condition. For example, it can result in inflammatory arthritis, problems affecting the nervous system and heart problems. It's better to wear long trousers rather than shorts in tick-infested country. Light clothing is better than dark clothing, because it's then easier to spot ticks and flick them off before they've managed to attach themselves to one's skin. If possible, avoid brushing past bracken or long grass, since ticks might be lurking there.

Dog owners in the UK should be aware of a potentially fatal canine disease that has befallen dogs exercised in the New Forest and other areas. There's some mystery concerning this illness, which seems to be 'Alabama rot' (also known as 'idiopathic cutaneous and renal glomerular vasculopathy') or something very similar.[7]

If you're used to walking though Britain's woodland, you may have come across litter, such as empty beer cans and bottles, and evidence of fires, indicating that irresponsible people have used the woods (most likely at night) for 'partying'. If you're planning a night-time woodland walk, it might be wise to avoid spots where such people congregate. My guess is that this sort of activity is much more likely to occur close to population centres than in more remote areas.

So far as brushes with the paranormal are concerned, I doubt whether walking through our woods and forests poses much physical risk. In Chapter 8, for instance, I've cited several witnesses who've reported unusual experiences in Rendlesham Forest, Suffolk. So far as I know, none of them experienced any significant deleterious after-effects. However, I'd like to sound a note of caution about close-encounter UFO experiences. Judging from the literature on the subject, getting close to UFOs (whatever their nature) *can* have harmful and disturbing effects. Therefore, my advice to anyone seeing, for example, a landed UFO in a forest clearing would be to observe it from a distance or to leave the scene altogether.

2

BAD VIBES IN A KENTISH WOOD

In the spring of 1969, a couple called Antony and Doreen Verney bought a property in Kent called Dargle Cottage. It's located about a mile and a half from the village of Biddenden and is approximately 10 miles west-south-west of Ashford. Most of the sources mentioned below state, *incorrectly*, that the cottage is *south-east* of Biddenden. In fact, it's more or less due south of it. The local authority is Ashford Borough Council.

The cottage is in a clearing within Sandpit Wood, which is part of a larger expanse of woodland. For fourteen years, the Verneys used it as a weekend retreat and holiday home. They retired in the summer of 1983. They temporarily rented their central London flat to a friend whose marriage had broken up, and they planned to make the cottage their main home. But in the autumn of 1983, their peace was reportedly disturbed by noises and vibrations; and strange lights lit up some nearby woods. They sought help from officialdom (the police, the local council, etc.), but allegedly received little or no assistance. Things escalated to a point where

Sandpit Wood, seen from Gribble Bridge Lane.

they decided to sell up. By the time they finally left, in May 1984, they were both suffering from significant health problems.

The couple died within months of each other, in 1996. I had no contact with them. In compiling this account, I've drawn on sources that differ from one another in minor respects. If what's described below is a close approximation to what really happened, the case is certainly a disturbing one. However, there are questions about the reliability of the testimony of the principal informant, Antony Verney.

MAIN SOURCES

PHILLIP CHAMBERLAIN

Phillip Chamberlain has worked as a freelance journalist. He currently heads the School of Film and Journalism at the University of the West of England, Bristol. It appears that he took up the Verneys' case in or around February 1992. At the time, he held office in the students' union of the University of Sussex and was still an undergraduate. A short account by him of the Verneys' experiences is available on the internet.[1] I emailed him in August 2018, enquiring whether he managed to get sight of any documents providing independent confirmation of what Mr Verney had reported, and I invited any additional comments. However, I received no reply.

'DR ARMEN VICTORIAN'

An excerpt from a book titled *Mind Controllers* is available on the internet from a man who was born as Habib Azadehdel in the former Soviet republic of Armenia.[2] He's perhaps better known as *Henry* Azadehdel, but he's used various aliases and has led a rather colourful life.[3] It seems that he gained the confidence of Mr Verney using the name 'Dr Armen Victorian', which he also uses in his book. Victorian's treatment of the case has a strong conspiracy-theory flavour but is quite detailed.

JUSTIN WILLIAMS

An account headed 'Nightmare at Dream Cottage' can be found in a 2011 book that's a compilation of stories.[4] Some of them originally appeared as a series of feature articles, referred to as Kent's 'X Files', in the *Kent Messenger* newspaper. Journalist Justin Williams was then working for the *Kent Messenger* and was involved in the articles. He and a colleague spent several months investigating Mr Verney's claims, both before and after publication of the feature about Dargle Cottage (which is referred to, pseudonymously, as 'Ivy Cottage' in the book). The account in the book presents Verney's story in neutral terms (i.e. it doesn't offer an opinion on whether his claims are historically true).

In 2018, I exchanged some email correspondence with Mr Williams, who kindly supplied me with copies of numerous documents bearing on the case. The quotations from Williams given below are from emails he sent me.

ANTONY VERNEY

Antony Verney is, of course, a central figure in this case. He's the named author of a twenty-eight-page booklet with the ironic title *The Happy Retirement*. Its subtitle reads: *How an old couples* [sic] *idyllic retirement cottage turned into a torture chamber, and who might have been responsible.* The title page gives a price of £1.20, but I don't know whether the booklet was ever formally published. It refers mainly to Verney and his wife in the third person. 'Verney's booklet', as I'll call it, is more detailed than either Victorian's book excerpt or Chamberlain's article, and its portrayal of what happened is different in some minor respects. On pp. 6–13, it reproduces an extensive log of events, recorded by Verney between late December 1983 and the second half of May 1984, when he and his wife finally left Dargle Cottage.

ALBERT BUDDEN

UFO researcher Albert Budden has written three books that examine links between anomalous experiences and exposure to magnetic and electric fields. One of them, *Psychic Close Encounters*, contains a short section on the Dargle Cottage case.[5] It seems that Budden communicated with Antony Verney. I was in touch with Budden some years ago, but I don't have his current contact details, and I've therefore been unable to ask him about his research into the case. However, his account of it adds little or nothing to what can be found in the aforementioned sources.

ANONYMOUS SOURCE

A person who wishes to remain anonymous has also given me some information pertaining to this case.

THE VERNEYS — BACKGROUND INFORMATION

I've gleaned the following information from various sources, some of which spell Mr Verney's first name, incorrectly, as 'Anthony' rather than as 'Antony'. He was born, as Harold Hill, on 27 December 1917, in Fulham, London. He was an actor as a teenager and young adult, and then a screenwriter, on and off, from his twenties. During the Second World War, he served in the Royal Air Force, in the signals section of Fighter Command. His television scripts included contributions to classic series such as *The Adventures of Robin Hood* and *No Hiding Place*, and he wrote the screenplay for the movie *You Lucky People*. His play *Trouble in the House* starred his wife and was staged at London's Cambridge Theatre. For some time, he served as a director of H.A. Percheron Ltd, which was established in 1898 by his wife's father, Henri. The business imported upmarket furnishing fabrics and wallpaper from France and, later, Italy. Leading interior designers were the principal client base. The company was eventually bought by one of its suppliers, Rubelli Ltd.

Antony Verney was a founder member of the Writers' Guild of Great Britain. For many years, he'd been an inspector for *The Good Food Guide*. According to his booklet, he also did work for the Consumers' Association with *The Good Hotel Guide* and was looking forward to expanding his interests in that field in his retirement, as well as returning to writing and forming a new company, to market his work. He died in London in September 1996, aged 78.

Doreen Julia Verney (née Percheron) was born on 12 April 1918 in Islington, London. She was the elder daughter of Henri Percheron and Jane Percheron (née Meale) and was an actress. During the Second World War, she served in the Entertainments National Service Association, which entertained members of the armed forces. She was also a director of H.A. Percheron. She died in Haywards Heath, West Sussex, in February 1996, aged 77.

The couple had a daughter, Eugenie. During the period that's the main focus of this chapter (September 1983–May 1984), she was working as a journalist and living in Derbyshire.

ALLEGED EVENTS AT THE COTTAGE

The following summary is a distillation based on the multiple sources I've mentioned. I've given particular weight to the Verney booklet, since it's quite detailed. I'm not aware of any documentation that provides independent corroboration of what Verney reported. That doesn't, of course, mean that no such evidence exists. For ease of expression, I'll be sparing in the use of 'distancing terminology' ('alleged', 'reported', etc.). I haven't attempted to mention every single incident or development, because that would probably make for tedious reading, given that the reported disturbances occurred very frequently and had a fairly consistent character.

SEPTEMBER 1983

Verney's booklet refers to a timber yard where doors and fencing were manufactured. It operated from 8 a.m. to 5 p.m. on weekdays and until 1 p.m. on Saturdays. (I presume that it was closed on Sundays.) The booklet describes it as being about three-quarters of a mile away from the cottage, to the north-west. However, I think it's referring to a site, still operational, that's about a third of a mile from the cottage, and almost due west of it. In early September 1983, there was a marked increase in noise from the site. At some point, Mr Verney spoke to the works manager, who showed concern. But when Verney spoke to the managing director, he was told that they were making no more noise than previously.

OCTOBER 1983

A visitor to Dargle Cottage noticed a strange humming noise coming up from the ground in the garden at the back of the building on 1 October. He took his dog for a walk in the woods, but it seemed ill at ease, and the woods seemed strangely silent, as if the wildlife had gone away. The birds didn't return to nest the following spring.

The humming persisted. On 5 October, the Verneys departed for a holiday in France, hoping that it would be gone by the time they returned. But when they got back, on 25 October, it was louder and was coming from all round the cottage. At times, in the early hours of the morning, it seemed to come from within the building, and had a throbbing and vibrating quality. The woods to the north-east would be lit up by yellow and pink lights, which appeared to be coming up from the ground. Also, the Verneys found that the drains associated with their kitchen sink had been blocked with pieces of broken asphalt. They had to be cleared by hand.

NOVEMBER 1983

By the beginning of November, the situation was worse. Although the humming had temporarily decreased, there was now a powerful throbbing noise, with a regular beat, which was accompanied by vibrations that seemed to come through the ground, affecting both the cottage and the surrounding area. The noise was apparently coming from a direction opposite to that of the timber yard (from the east, presumably), and was loudest in the early hours of the morning. During working hours, when it was less intense, sounds from the timber yard often masked it.

The noise got progressively worse during November. Deprived of sleep night after night, the couple were becoming irritable with each other, and were experiencing problems with their short-term memory. Wondering whether the problem was related to a water pump or some type of agricultural activity, the Verneys contacted local water authorities but were told that they had no facilities in the area that could be responsible.

The couple would go out at night and attempt to locate the source of the noise. But its point of origin seemed to move around. About 1 a.m. on 24 November, they encountered a police patrol. The two officers were able to hear the noise and thought it might be coming from Short's Wood.[6] (Three of the sources – Verney's booklet, Victorian's book excerpt and the book *Unexplained Kent* – give the direction as 'north-east'. But that's presumably wrong, since Short's Wood is actually *south-east* of Dargle Cottage.) The police officers said they'd report it and would let the couple know if they managed to find the source. But when Mr Verney visited Tenterden police station on 26 November, a sergeant informed him that no report had been lodged and that it wasn't a police matter. The officer said that it was the responsibility of the council's environmental health department. But he added that they were 'bloody useless'! Two days later, Verney phoned them. He explained the nature of the problem to a secretary, and left his number, but his call wasn't returned.

On 1 December, the couple went away for a few days to visit their daughter in Derbyshire, principally to get some respite from what Verney's booklet describes as the 'electronic pollution'. When they returned, on 6 December, there were no messages on their answerphone from the environmental health department. They left further messages but still didn't get a reply. A letter sent to the environmental health officer (EHO) also went unanswered. Mr Verney wrote to the borough treasurer's department, asking for a reduction in rates, given the pollution. The Verneys also wrote to the council's planning department, asking whether permission had been given for something that might have been the cause of the trouble, but the enquiry didn't bear fruit.

To make matters worse, during the weekend of 17/18 December, the couple's electricity supply fluctuated for no obvious reason. Mr Verney contacted the supply company. According to Verney's booklet, around 8 a.m. on 20 December there were about eight men in the woods, working on the power lines; and two large trucks and two vans were present. (However, Chamberlain's article refers to some six vehicles, whereas Victorian's book excerpt mentions just 'two vans'.) The electricity supply improved, but the lighting continued to fluctuate for some weeks. On 19 and 20 December, the supply company's chief engineer for the area, a Mr Green, spoke of placing instruments in the cottage, to take readings. That was supposed to have happened after Christmas, but nothing more was heard from him.

Mr Verney contacted a firm of acoustic engineers in Maidstone on 20 December, and a Mr Bassett made a visit that evening. Because of bad weather, the noise was hard to hear. But Bassett reportedly obtained a very strong instrumental reading in respect of vibrations.[7] He declared that the source was less than a mile from the cottage, and that he would relay his findings to the council's EHO. (Judging from p. 6 of Verney's booklet, it was actually a colleague of Bassett's who spoke to the EHO. That happened on the following day, 21 December. On 29 December, Mr Verney spoke to Bassett's colleague, who said that during his conversation with the EHO several days earlier, the latter had suggested that the Maidstone-based firm should take no further action, since he, the EHO, would do all he could to help the Verneys, given that he was empowered by the Control of Pollution Act and possessed the necessary instruments to do the job.)

On the afternoon of 21 December, the EHO finally rang. He was reportedly unforthcoming and wouldn't promise to take action under the Control of Pollution Act. He said that he couldn't do anything until after Christmas. According to Verney, the EHO rejected the suggestion of putting equipment in the cottage to obtain readings, claiming that he had no instruments; and he seemed to think it improper when Verney offered to obtain them himself. At his wife's urging, Verney rang the EHO again the next day, asking for help before the start of the Christmas holidays. But, again, the response was discouraging.

In desperation, Mr Verney travelled to London, to enquire about hiring some recording equipment. However, this part of the story puzzles me a little, because – as explained above – Mr Bassett of the Maidstone-based company had *already* visited the cottage and had supposedly obtained a strong reading confirming the presence of vibrations. Anyway, at an electrical shop in Tottenham Court Road, it was suggested to Verney that the Ministry of Defence (MoD) might be responsible for the problems. He was introduced to a John Dyus,[8] described as a 'leading electronic scientist', who offered to visit the cottage after Christmas.

The idea of MoD involvement hadn't occurred to Verney before, but it made sense to him, given the EHO's behaviour and the reluctance of the local police to pursue the matter. And, according to Verney's booklet, the MoD wouldn't have been subject to the Control of Pollution Act or any other civil law.

Verney's booklet (p. 4) states that a near neighbour explained that work had taken place in the Short's Wood/Gribble Wood area two or three years previously, involving bulldozers, heavy lorries and earth-moving machinery. Although trees were felled in a large area, nothing had been built above ground there.

The Verneys had begun to suspect that their phone was being tapped. A recently built house (bungalow would be a better word), a little over half a mile away in a roughly easterly direction, caught Mr Verney's attention. It was supposedly of unusual construction[9] and surrounded by high hedges. Judging from Chamberlain's article, this was October Farm, but it would be more accurate to describe the building as a *part of* October Farm. According to the planning application submitted to the local council (which I have seen, courtesy of Justin Williams), it was to be the residence of the proprietors, who – it seems – may have been living in a mobile home on the farm. In other words, there may be no mystery about why permission was sought to build the bungalow.

Verney discovered that it was occupied by a couple in their forties. Although planning documents referred to a farm, there was no sign of any agricultural activity, apart from some beehives. According to Verney's booklet (pp. 4–5), at the front of the building, and running down the side of it for a distance, there was some sort of bunker, which was thought locally to be a septic tank. It had an air vent shaped like a mushroom. Chamberlain's article states that the bunker was covered with grass. Opaque, floor-length net curtains blocked the view into the ground floor windows of the house. Victorian's book excerpt and Verney's booklet (p. 4) state that the curtains were made from a textile manufactured exclusively for the Department of the Environment's Property Services Agency and used to protect high-security buildings. One might wonder how the fabric could be identified so precisely, although on at least one occasion, Christmas Eve, Mr Verney used binoculars to view the building. He was confronted by the female occupant, described in Verney's booklet as a large woman 'with the air of somebody used to authority'. He mentioned the problem affecting his home, and she suggested that the noise must have been coming from the timber yard. Chamberlain quotes her as adding, 'We breed Dobermans here, you know.' She said that she would ask her husband whether he had any thoughts as to the source of the problem, and Verney gave her his phone number.

In what could be seen as indicative of paranoia, the Verneys thought it was too much of a coincidence that the property was called October Farm, given that their troubles had begun in October.[10] Chamberlain states that Verney took to referring to 'Operation October' in his correspondence with Ashford Borough Council! Chamberlain notes that that may have had a curious effect: the swinging sign 'To October Farm' was replaced with one reading 'To Orchard Farm'. However, I visited the area in October 2018 and noticed that the property is still called October Farm.

There's a pitch-and-putt golf course adjacent to the farm. The former *Kent Messenger* reporter Justin Williams noted: 'We went to October Farm and met its owner. … The owner allowed us to look around and I can assure you there was absolutely nothing sinister about the place.' Williams believes that the couple at the farm had a smallholding there, and he's fairly sure that they owned the pitch and putt when it opened. He thinks they stopped farming at that point. He explained that, 'There was no bunker and we could not find the air vent that Verney claimed he had seen.' However, since this visit occurred some years after the Verneys had left the area, it's possible that a structure with an air vent had been removed at some point. Williams' impression was that Verney had been viewed as a pest and that the owner of the property was thoroughly sick of the subsequent attention from the UFO community. Williams added:

> We spoke to the people who owned Biddenden Vineyards on Gribble Bridge Lane.[11] They had been there since the late 60s/ early 70s and their land abuts Shorts Wood and October Farm. They said that they had never witnessed anything strange to back up Verney's claims.
>
> Shorts Wood was coppiced pretty regularly and would have been managed during the 80s. It strikes me as a rather unlikely place to site some kind of secret facility.

Victorian's book excerpt quotes Verney as stating that around that time (late 1983), the nights at Dargle Cottage were awful, 'with lots of activity with the lights *in* and around the house' (my emphasis).

At first light on Boxing Day, Mr Verney noticed a new phenomenon, which he recorded in a log that he started keeping: three lit-up, horseshoe-shaped objects crossed the sky. They were going from west to east (according to Victorian's book excerpt and p. 6 of Verney's booklet) or north-west to south-east (according to Chamberlain). Verney likened them to 'flying tiaras' and he noted that they disappeared while losing height over the Short's Wood/Gribble Wood area. Verney's booklet (p. 19) notes that a borough councillor called Mrs Hawksley claimed to have seen pink lights in the locality on more than one occasion. The booklet (p. 10) also states that a purportedly senior colleague of the aforementioned EHO told Verney (on 20 January 1984) that members of the public had informed his department about UFO sightings in the area.

Feeling unrested and very ill as a result of what was happening, the couple went away to a hotel in East Sussex on 27 December. They sought a new home in that area and found a house to their liking the very next day. After checking out of the hotel on 29 December, they revisited the property they were interested in and made a firm offer to buy it. When they returned to the cottage, their torment continued more or less continuously, day after day.

EARLY 1984

In a new development, Mr Verney claimed that he and his wife were 'zapped' by some sort of 'electronic beam' around 3 a.m. on 5 January 1984. It reportedly made no noise, but it caused excruciating pain at the top of the head and in the temples. There were to be further such 'zappings'.

On 6 January, the EHO showed up and reportedly behaved very strangely. He refused to enter the house. Instead of adopting a normal pose in speaking to Mr Verney, he stood at his side, speaking out of the corner of his mouth. He declined to take any action about the noise pollution. After taking some twelve steps down the side of the cottage, he stood on the grass, staring at the woods, jingling money in his pockets. A couple of minutes later, he said that he couldn't hear any noise. He again refused to place recording devices in the house and then left. However, Verney's log (p. 8) notes that the noise wasn't 'running' at the time, although it resumed in the early afternoon but wasn't very loud. (A recurrent feature of the alleged disturbances was that when other people were on site, there was a tendency for things to be quiet. This gave the Verneys the impression that they were under surveillance and that those responsible for the disturbances could turn them on and off at will. I'll refer to this as the *switch-off effect*.)

Chamberlain notes that the EHO made two subsequent visits to the cottage, each time behaving in the same odd way. Verney's booklet indicates that there were nights when he, Verney, rang the council's duty officer and requested a visit from the EHO, who failed to turn up.

According to Verney's booklet (p. 8), there was a temporary reversal of the usual pattern on 6/7 January: after the quietest night for weeks, a hum, thumping and vibrations began at 7 a.m. on the 7th, becoming very noisy as the day passed. The disturbances continued into the early hours of the next day.

On 9 January, Mr Verney went to London to see Mr Dyus, the electronics expert he'd met in London the previous month. Sound recordings made at the cottage were run through Dyus's equipment.

Verney's log for 15 January noted that in the early morning, the humming and vibrating were the 'worst ever', that he was 'zapped' again by the supposed energy beam, and that lights were going up and down (in the trees, presumably). Verney got dressed and went out in his car. There was an overall humming, and he reportedly saw a UFO flying under a cloud with its lights flashing on and off.

On 18 January, Verney collected Dyus in London and drove him to Kent for a visit to the cottage. On the way, they called in at a pub in Biddenden for lunch. While they were there, Verney's car was broken into, and his cheque book and latest bank statement were stolen.[12] At the cottage, the switch-off effect manifested itself again: no noise or vibrations were evident. About ten minutes after their arrival, the EHO appeared, although Verney hadn't told the council about Dyus's impending visit. This time, the EHO did enter the cottage. Somehow, he knew Dyus's name, and the sight of the latter's equipment seemed to make the EHO uneasy. He questioned Dyus about what he was going to do and where he was from. Then, he asked Verney to go outside with him, where he returned, without comment, some tapes of noise recordings left at his office the previous week.[13]

A bandage on one of the EHO's fingers extended some way beyond the digit itself. Dyus wondered whether it concealed a two-way radio device. Victorian's book excerpt notes that the Joint Intelligence Training Unit at Ashford would have been in possession of such an item in 1984.

Shortly before the EHO departed, there was suddenly a flurry of sound from the timber yard, causing him to declare that he'd never heard it so loud.

Mr Dyus lowered a rifle-microphone into a well outside the front of the cottage. Notwithstanding the switch-off effect, it supposedly detected a high level of vibrations, which must have been travelling through the ground. (Evidently, though, the vibrations weren't strong enough to be felt by Dyus and the Verneys.) Although Dyus stayed for several hours, the noise remained mysteriously absent. Verney drove him back to London and didn't return until the next day. The noise and vibrations at the cottage resumed about half an hour after the men departed, and Mrs Verney went on to have what she described as her worst night yet.

Verney's log for 20 January states that banging sounds were heard from about 1.30 p.m., coming from the woods to the north-east. They continued, at regular intervals of three minutes, until 5.30 p.m. According to Chamberlain, the woman from October Farm rang Verney around 3 p.m. Seemingly very concerned, she asked whether he could hear the bangs. However, the call was cut off, and when Verney phoned directory inquiries, he was told that they had no number for the farm.

According to Verney's booklet (p. 11), the last visit from the EHO occurred on 24 January. This time, the switch-off effect didn't manifest itself. Noise and vibrations were present, and fairly strong, but the EHO claimed that he couldn't hear anything. Subsequently, on two occasions, he rang about 7 p.m. and offered to come and hear the noise. But on the first occasion, there was a gale and torrential rain, which would have made it hard to hear anything; and on the second occasion, there was a lull in the noise disturbance. (The booklet suggests that the EHO may have known that when making the call. It also remarks that in the course of his dealings with the Verneys, the EHO never mentioned the vibrations.)

Verney's booklet (p. 19) states that the inhabitants of the nearest house, over a quarter of a mile away, in Short's Wood, had complained of hearing the humming, and had experienced continual interference with their television reception in the evening hours. The booklet also mentions a couple living in a Portakabin, further away in Short's Wood. They'd reportedly been troubled by the noise, and with fluctuations in their lighting.

SPRING 1984

After being away from the cottage for a period, the Verneys returned on 16 March and soon discovered that there was a blockage related to their septic tank. When the drains were dug out, it was found that, in one section, concrete had been inserted into the pipes, presumably during their absence.

The couple put the cottage up for sale in March. Verney's booklet (p. 19) indicates that when would-be buyers came to view the property, there was no disturbing activity. Sale of the cottage was made on 2 April, with a completion date of 24 May.

On 5 April, the Verneys were telephoned at their London flat by a Detective Constable George Keeler of the Ashford CID, who explained that a window had been broken at their Kent cottage, although no one seemed to have actually entered the premises. The Verneys returned to the cottage the next day, and discovered that there *had* been a break-in, although nothing of value had been stolen, except some papers relating to Mr Verney's tax affairs, and (according to Victorian) some letters from a friend of the family (a Privy Counsellor and former Cabinet minister). Part of a bar of chocolate was also missing. I've been informed that an old typewriter, of sentimental value to Mr Verney, was also taken.

Victorian's book excerpt assumes that when the police noticed the broken window, they failed to make a proper check, and hence missed the fact that there'd been a break-in. (However, it's conceivable that the break-in occurred shortly *after* the police inspected the window.) Verney's booklet (p. 12) goes further, suggesting that the police hadn't even visited the premises, and that DC Keeler must have been 'under instructions' when he phoned the Verneys in London to inform them about the broken window!

At some point in April or May, Mr Dyus made another visit to Dargle Cottage, but it seems that the switch-off effect manifested itself again.

Verney's booklet explains that his daughter (Eugenie) and a colleague of hers came for the weekend on 18 May, to help with the packing for the impending move. Things were quiet until the early hours of 20 May. About 1 a.m. that day, Mr Verney woke with an intense burning feeling in his eyes. It subsided, but the noise and vibrations started around 1.30 a.m. The booklet claims (pp. 12–13) that 'all hell was let loose', the disturbances continuing, non-stop, until after 7 a.m. Lights were seen and bangs were heard. The 'zapper' was deployed again, although the booklet doesn't say who was targeted by it. Eugenie reportedly stated that she was terrified, and that she'd heard men shouting in the woods. However, her friend slept through all this. Later that day, at a party in London involving some of her old school friends, Eugenie was reportedly unable to remember any of their names. The booklet states that she suffered from memory problems for about a week and was off work. It also states that her colleague was taken ill on the M1 motorway but was able to pull into the car park of a service station before passing out. (The implication presumably is that after leaving the cottage, Eugenie and her friend drove to London and later headed back to Derbyshire.)

Chamberlain's article and Victorian's book excerpt describe the events of that weekend slightly differently.

POSSIBLE EFFECTS ON MR AND MRS VERNEY'S HEALTH

In June 1983, a few months prior to their bad experiences at the cottage, the Verneys underwent medical examinations at Tenterden Health Centre in connection with a pension scheme. Records reportedly showed that they came through the tests very well. Alas, though, both of them soon experienced serious health problems. However, as noted below, it might be wrong to attribute all of these difficulties to what they experienced at Dargle Cottage.

ANTONY VERNEY

Mr Verney was very unwell during a period of three weeks in February and March 1984. He experienced pains in his back and thighs, and he had difficulty in walking and staying upright. The pain was more or less continuous, and he found it difficult to sleep or rest. Medical tests in March showed abnormalities. Between March and May 1984, he lost most of his teeth: some fell out, and others simply crumbled.

X-rays indicated permanent damage to Verney's lower lumbar region and spinal area. Blood abnormalities persisted for more than three years. He experienced three severe attacks of something resembling shingles, and he was also troubled by pains in his limbs. He also had to endure recurrent episodes of swelling of his nipples, which could be painful.

Verney's booklet (p. 22) refers to minor surgery that Mr Verney underwent: a suspected basal cell carcinoma (a type of skin cancer) was removed in July 1989; and another suspected basal cell carcinoma was removed in January 1990. However, the booklet states that these diagnoses proved incorrect, although doctors were unable to identify the nature and cause of the lesions. If they *were* forms of skin cancer, they may have been unrelated to anything that happened at Dargle Cottage. Unprotected exposure to strong sunlight is a recognised risk factor for skin cancer, and Mr Verney had spent a lot of time in the sunny Mediterranean area over the years.

As noted above, Mr Verney died in September 1996, aged 78. According to Victorian, Verney had checked himself into a psycho-geriatric ward, against the advice of family and friends, apparently hoping that he would get relief from microwave pollution.

DOREEN VERNEY

Mrs Verney suffered two attacks of severe stomach cramps and vomiting in January and February 1984. She remained unwell throughout March, but tests in April apparently failed to identify anything serious. But she and her husband may have become sensitised to electromagnetic influences while at the cottage. For example, during a road trip that they made to Scotland at the end of January 1984, Mrs Verney believed that she could sense electrical junction boxes more than a quarter of a mile away.

When the couple moved out of the cottage on 23 May, Mrs Verney was experiencing severe pain in her legs and lumbar region, and she was barely able to walk, although further medical tests failed to identify the cause.

Four of the sources I've cited (Chamberlain, Victorian, Verney's booklet and *Unexplained Kent*) state that Mrs Verney was admitted to the Fitzroy Nuffield Hospital in London at the end of August 1984, where a rare form of lymphatic leukaemia was diagnosed.[14] However, my understanding is that this is incorrect, and that the condition diagnosed was, in fact, ovarian cancer. She underwent surgery on 1 September and then had two months of chemotherapy.

Although she pulled through her cancer treatment, Mrs Verney had become a semi-invalid, and she experienced a lot of pain. Unfortunately, she suffered a stroke in June 1991 and became a resident in a care home for the elderly. She died in February 1996 following another stroke. She was six weeks short of her 78th birthday.

FURTHER DEVELOPMENTS

It seems that the Verneys left no forwarding address when they moved out of the cottage; and because of a misspelling of Mr Verney's name on his driving licence, the couple felt that they couldn't be traced to their new house. They posted any mail related to 'Operation October' well outside their new postal area. On 1 October 1984, Mr Verney sent a letter, by recorded delivery, to William Whitelaw, the Deputy Prime Minister. Some ten days later, someone called at the sub-post office concerned, asking about Verney's address. On 1 November that year, Verney noticed a couple of uniformed policemen examining his car. When he opened his door and asked what they were doing, he was given an implausible explanation. Shortly after, while he was away in London, visiting his wife in hospital, the house was broken into. Chamberlain refers to 'years of harassment, break-ins and interference with the mail and telephone'. He states that Verney blamed it on Willy Whitelaw!

Mr Verney exchanged a lot of correspondence with 'officialdom'. At one point, he received a letter from an MoD official, denying any MoD involvement and attributing the Verneys' problems to 'the activities of criminal elements in the area', which was a matter for the civil police. Verney sent a copy of the letter to the Chief Constable of Kent, and then several reminders. In early March 1987, he was contacted by an Inspector Watkins of the Kent police. An appointment was made. Two weeks later, Watkins and a colleague visited Verney. Watkins explained that he'd called on the MoD official, asking him to provide evidence for his statement about 'criminal elements in the area'. But the person was apparently non-committal. The visiting police officers were reportedly horri-fied by the 'recordings' that had been made at Dargle Cottage. (I presume that Verney played them some audio-recordings.) At the end of the meeting (which lasted ninety minutes or more), Verney asked Watkins for his opinion. He allegedly attributed the Verneys' ordeal to the activities of an organisation over which the Kent police had no jurisdiction. Verney subsequently sought written confirmation of the inspector's statement, but didn't get it.

Verney's communications with the authorities weren't entirely confined to the dark chapter that began in the autumn of 1983 at Dargle Cottage. In March 1996, he wrote to the House of Lords office of Lady Margaret Thatcher, who'd previously (1979–90) been Prime Minister of the UK. As well as referring to the attack on him and his wife by 'a galaxy of Cold War weaponry' in Kent and suggesting that Thatcher should be put on trial, he referred to September 1975, when he was in the United States on a business trip. He'd been trying to secure investment that would have created manufacturing jobs in the UK. Thatcher was then leader of the Conservative opposition. Verney claimed that speeches by her in the USA, bad-mouthing the UK, had deterred the hoped-for investment, and had left him personally out of pocket. The letter indicated that, taking everything into account, he expected a million pounds in compensation from the Thatcher Foundation, plus three million pounds from the government (in recompense for the events that began at Dargle Cottage)!

The aforementioned letter to Lady Thatcher's office at the House of Lords was written from an address in Hassocks, West Sussex. This seems to have been a flat that was adjacent to the nursing home where Doreen Verney had resided. I presume that Mr Verney moved there from Streat, East Sussex, to be closer to her. The letter stated that he'd had two electronics experts check the exterior of the flat, and that it was in an electromagnetic field, with the beams entering part of the nursing home and going into the bedroom in which his recently deceased wife had languished.[15] He surmised that 'she has been pursued from her beloved house in Kent to the doors of the crematorium.'

SUBSEQUENT OWNERS OF DARGLE COTTAGE

Unexplained Kent (p. 52) refers to 'later owners' of Dargle Cottage who had moved there in the late 1980s and who had had no strange experiences, apart from some bother with 'researchers' into the Verney case creeping around in the woods. If these owners did indeed move there in the *late* 1980s, the cottage must have changed hands at least twice in that decade. It would be interesting to know whether the person or persons who bought the property from the Verneys in 1984 were troubled by noises, vibrations and strange lights.

Justin Williams explained that:

> Several 'investigators' ... visited Dargle Cottage in the 1990s and threatened to dig up the patio 'to see what is underneath'. The owners called the police. I think [they] were pestered for some time.

In April 2013, I wrote to 'The Householder' at Dargle Cottage, referring to reports concerning the Verneys' occupancy. I explained that I didn't know whether any subsequent owners or occupiers had experienced anything unusual there. I said: 'If you're able to provide any relevant information, I'd be most grateful.' Perhaps not surprisingly, I received no reply.

COMMENTS

To a degree, there's nothing exceptional about aspects of the Verneys' reported experiences. In their book *Modern Mysteries of Britain*, Janet and Colin Bord (p. 186) noted that there were many press reports in the 1970s and early 1980s about people being plagued by a continuous, unidentifiable humming noise. The Bords pointed out that the sufferers described it as having a throbbing quality, like the idling of a lorry engine. They quoted a Paul Wallace of Poole, Dorset, who – by 1972 – had been hearing it for five years. He referred to it as 'a ringing hum, a vibration which is very painful'. He related that it gave him headaches and migraine and prevented him from getting a good night's sleep. He added that his hearing was 'A1', and that the noise was faint or non-existent when he was out of the area. The Bords noted (p. 188) that cases had been found going back to 1727.

Over the years, 'the hum' has been experienced far and wide – for example, in Bristol (western England), Largs (western Scotland), Sudbury (eastern England), Kokomo (Indiana, USA) and Taos (New Mexico, USA). With some people who hear it, there could be medical explanations. Where the cause is definitely external, there's a wide range of possibilities, including, for example, aircraft noise, extremely low-frequency communication signals, seismic activity, and vibration of the ocean floor. According to a short 2004 article by Mark Pilkington, a low hum in Kokomo (USA) was traced to industrial fans in a factory.[16] A website attributes the phenomenon to 'gravitational waves' generated by high-voltage electrical supply grids interacting with charged particles in the ionosphere, and it suggests that the hum isn't a sound as such, but rather an effect produced in the percipient by the gravitational waves.[17]

In the above-mentioned cases (e.g. that of the 'Bristol hum') there are, or have been, multiple witnesses. But in the case of Dargle Cottage, there seem to have been very few witnesses apart from Mr and Mrs Verney.

WERE THE VERNEYS DELIBERATELY TARGETED?

If, despite the lack of supporting evidence, we conjecture that there may be some truth in the Verneys' story, could it be that they just happened to be in the wrong place at the wrong time? Was some sort of covert project or experiment in progress, without there being any intention to cause the couple distress? On that basis, one might surmise that when Mr Verney started asking awkward questions, those behind the operation increased the disturbances (noises, vibrations, etc.) and employed additional tactics (e.g. breaking into his car) in an attempt to silence him and induce the couple to leave Dargle Cottage. However, as early as October 1983 – *before* the Verneys started contacting the authorities – the couple allegedly discovered that the drains associated with their kitchen sink had been blocked with pieces of broken asphalt. Therefore, assuming that the incident with the blocked drains truly occurred, it seems more likely that they'd been targeted from the outset, although the reason isn't clear. The scale of what was supposedly happening seems to rule out the possibility that a private individual – e.g. a disaffected relative or a former business associate – was pursuing a vendetta, unless we're to assume that the supposed culprit had access to expensive and sophisticated equipment and a considerable power source.

Could it be that the Verneys were used as guinea pigs for the testing of some dastardly military technology designed to deprive people of sleep and make them unwell? If so, it's conceivable that they were targeted because their home was in a secluded area, with the woods providing good cover for the perpetrators.

Of course, all of this is highly conjectural. However, there have been other reports concerning supposed 'sonic attacks'. Writing in an online *Scientific American* article in February 2018, R. Douglas Fields, a neuroscientist, referred to recent heated exchanges between the USA and Cuba. They related to a supposed attack on employees at the American embassy in Havana by some form of sonic weapon, thought to have been trained on them mainly at their residences.[18] Cuba denied that such a thing had taken place. But both sides acknowledged bafflement about what had happened to twenty-four embassy staff between November 2016 and August 2017. A study carried out by doctors at the University of Pennsylvania examined twenty-one of the US government employees, and found that they'd experienced concussion-like symptoms, which varied widely among them. They included cognitive difficulties, and problems with balance, eye tracking, sleep disturbance and headaches. But their MRI brain scans were normal. Except in the case of three of them, their hearing was also normal. The authors of the study discounted the likelihood of sonic injury, infection or toxic agents, and downplayed the suggestion that the employees had succumbed to 'mass hysteria'. Fields notes that many of the findings echo those of a previous investigation by Cuban officials.

The September 2018 issue of the magazine *Fortean Times* explained that some employees at the US consulate in Guangzhou, China, had experienced similar problems.[19] But a recent study suggests that sounds heard by the afflicted embassy staff in Havana may have been produced by insects – Indies short-tailed crickets.[20] However, this may not account for all of their reported problems.

As noted, the alleged phenomena in the Dargle Cottage case included strange light effects and UFO sightings. One might have expected that Mr Verney would try to photograph those manifestations, but I don't recall seeing any mention of photos in what I've read about the case. If these phenomena were real, it's conceivable that they entailed holographic projections, the use of drones, or some other type of advanced technology.

WAS THIS AN ATYPICAL POLTERGEIST OR HAUNTING CASE?

The word 'poltergeist' comes from German words meaning 'noisy spirit', although *Spukphenome* is the preferred term in Germany itself. Poltergeist cases entail recurrent physical phenomena, such as the movement of objects, rapping and knocking sounds, and the breakage of glass and crockery. Poltergeist phenomena tend to be person-centred, and may be generated, unconsciously, by the 'focal' person. The term 'haunting' or 'haunt' is applied to cases featuring recurrent manifestations, of an apparently paranormal nature, that seem to be linked with particular places rather than specific people. Although clear-cut physical phenomena are reported in many haunt cases, the manifestations are sometimes wholly, or predominantly, of a sensory character (sights, sounds, tactile impressions, etc.). In practice, it's not always easy to decide whether a case should be considered a poltergeist episode or a haunting. In terms of the underlying mechanisms, there may be a lot of overlap.

With poltergeists and hauntings, there's often a mischievous, tricksterish character to the phenomena. Take, for instance, a case that I investigated in Scotland some years ago. One of the informants mentioned an occasion when he discovered that three folded £20 notes had disappeared from a metal container in his living room. When he returned to his house at lunchtime that day, three £20 notes were laid out on the coffee table! They appeared new and weren't creased. However, the manifestations that allegedly occurred at Dargle Cottage between October 1983 and May 1984 were more intense and sustained than those in a typical poltergeist outbreak or haunting: it seems that the disturbing vibrations and sounds sometimes continued, non-stop, for very long periods. Furthermore, the character of the phenomena was different from that in typical poltergeist or haunt cases. In the latter, for example, people might report hearing footsteps, sensing a presence, or fleetingly seeing an apparitional figure. None of these things seems to have been reported at Dargle Cottage. Therefore, if we're to class it as a haunting, it's a pretty unusual one.

PSYCHOLOGICAL FACTORS

Consciously or unconsciously, there may have been a degree of exaggeration or embellishment in Mr Verney's reporting. The anonymous source I referred to above believes that was the case.

If the events occurred as described by Mr Verney, it's not surprising that he and his wife felt harassed and persecuted. However, it's worth asking whether a pre-existing tendency to interpret events in a paranoid way played a role in their experiences. As noted above, on seemingly slender grounds, the couple came to suspect that some sort of covert activity was going on at October Farm and was behind their troubles. They even saw something of sinister significance in the name of the property, given that their problems had begun in the month of October (if we disregard the fact that they'd been bothered by noise from the timber yard the previous month). As also noted above, Mr Verney started referring to 'Operation October' in his correspondence with Ashford Borough Council. He evidently thought there was some sort of conspiracy afoot, and he may have given council employees the impression that they were dealing with a crank. Paradoxically, that may have encouraged them to take his complaints less seriously. At any rate, since he was in a psychiatric ward at the end of his life, we can reasonably infer that his mental health wasn't good then.

Justin Williams, the former *Kent Messenger* journalist, informed me that he met Antony Verney two or three times in the mid 1990s (which would have been shortly before Verney's death). He explains:

> At the time, we were writing a series of colourful features about unexplained phenomena and thoroughly enjoying the buzz. Some of them ... were particularly interesting and did raise

some fascinating questions. It was in this atmosphere that we approached the Verney story – we very much wanted it to be true.

However, on the basis of his and his colleague's enquiries, Williams came to sceptical conclusions about the case. On one occasion, he visited Verney at his home in Hassocks. Verney claimed that he'd just suffered a break-in by the security services. But it was clear to Williams at the time that Verney had simply imagined that. Williams notes:

> Sadly, the Verney story was celebrated among a group of people who described themselves as 'investigators'. Some of these people were responsible for filling Verney's head with some of his more extraordinary claims.
>
> During the course of our investigations we tracked down anybody still alive and traceable who had been mentioned by Verney, including the sound engineer and a policeman who had worked in Tenterden at the time. After talking to these witnesses, it was clear that there was absolutely nothing to substantiate anything that Verney claimed.[21] I do have a file filled with letters and other documents ... but nothing in it proves anything or even suggests that the germ of Verney's paranoia was grounded in fact.

Williams is convinced that the events at Dargle Cottage described by Verney didn't occur, although there may possibly have been some dispute over noise involving a saw mill several hundred metres away in Short's Wood. But whatever happened in respect of that, he doesn't think it had a sinister origin.

Justin Williams may be right in his conclusions. But caution is warranted, since his contacts with Mr Verney occurred shortly before the latter's death. It may be that Verney was a lot less paranoid in the autumn of 1983, when his problems at Dargle Cottage began. Furthermore, a susceptibility to delusions on Verney's part doesn't, in itself, rule out the possibility that something genuinely strange was going on in 1983/4. Indeed, if that was the case, the events may have ratcheted up any pre-existing paranoia.

As for the frustrations that the Verneys experienced in dealing with 'officialdom', there could be prosaic, non-conspiratorial explanations for at least some of the problems they encountered. For example, delays in receiving replies to letters and phone calls may have been a reflection of organisational inefficiency, inadequate staff training and laziness on the part of certain employees.

Despite his sceptical conclusions, Williams notes:

[T]here were a number of loose ends and open questions with the case. I was concerned about the circumstances surrounding Verney's death, the fact that a locum who we could not track down had referred him to a psychiatric unit and the administration of a powerful anti-psychotic which a friendly physician had said was highly unusual given that nobody had ever believed Verney was a threat to himself. Also, later [after publication of the *Kent Messenger* article] the female owner of Dargle Cottage had called me to say that somebody had poisoned their goats. I also believe that her husband may have contracted some form of lymphoma, although I'm hazy on this. Nothing concrete, all just little details which added to my unease with it.

If Williams is right in thinking that a locum doctor referred Antony Verney to a psychiatric unit, it slightly contradicts the assertion, in Victorian's book excerpt, that Verney 'had *checked himself* into a psycho-geriatric ward' (my emphasis). Regarding the reported poisoning of goats, Williams notes that it's conceivable that 'somebody who had been sent packing from Dargle Cottage (maybe one of those who pestered the couple about digging on their land) could have been responsible for the alleged poisoning, as retribution for being turned away.'

3

THE GOREBRIDGE LIGHTS

Gorebridge is a former coal-mining village in the county of Midlothian in east-central Scotland. As the crow flies, it's about 10 miles south-south-east of the centre of Edinburgh. It gets its name from the bridge across the River Gore, a tributary of the River South Esk. In terms of size, it could be classed as a small town, with a population of about 6,500. It appears ordinary enough, albeit a bit drab and grey, although there are some places of historical interest nearby, such as Dalhousie Castle, which is now a hotel.

The village has experienced problems related to its coal mining past. In 2013, a family living in Newbyres Crescent were affected by carbon dioxide that was thought to be seeping into their home from abandoned coal workings beneath them. That eventually led to the evacuation of people from sixty-four homes in Newbyres Crescent and nearby Gore Avenue, and the subsequent demolition of the properties, which lacked the protective gas membranes required for buildings constructed over former mine workings.[1] In September 2016, four families from nearby Newbyres Avenue were also moved out because of excessive carbon dioxide in their homes.[2]

To the north-east of Gorebridge, there's a long, wooded hill. Much of it is named Camp Wood, probably because there was a Roman fort or encampment there centuries ago. Locals refer to the area as 'the camp'. It can be reached via two narrow minor roads (see the map opposite). I'll call them *Roads A* and *B*. Road A runs past the north-eastern end of Camp Wood. Road B, about one and a quarter miles to the south-west, marks the south-western boundary of Camp Wood. The woodland south-west of Road B is known as Common Wood. Judging from the amount of refuse strewn beside it, Road B is used by fly-tippers.

Main Street, Gorebridge.

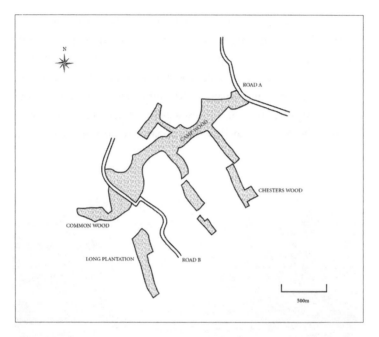

Camp Wood.

ALLEGED PHENOMENA

Andrew Hennessey runs Stargate Edinburgh Tours, a company that provides guided excursions to places associated with paranormal lore, including the Gorebridge area.[3] His parents hail from the village, so he has a personal connection with it. He claims that the general area is a very active hot spot for anomalous phenomena, and that the camp is the site of an alien base! Items by him concerning Gorebridge can be found on the internet[4]. He also discusses the area's alleged weirdness in his 2017 book *Alien Encounters and the Paranormal: The Scottish Experience*. The page numbers cited below relate to it.

Hennessey states that there've been reports of walkers seeing strange lights and activity at night among the trees at the camp since at least the 1970s (p. 42). The article referenced in Note 4 mentions, among other things, a couple of unnamed local men who were there one unspecified night, trying to collect pine trees – illegally, I presume – to sell as Christmas trees. They were reportedly chased away by what appeared to be a huge, glowing, green eye.

Path through Camp Wood.

Hennessey's book explains that he photographed several glowing UFOs at the camp in the summer of 2010 (p. 42). Some of them seemed to be about 6 feet wide. They would float above the trees for a few seconds, with their glow intensifying and their form becoming less distinct. Then, they would suddenly disappear. He relates (p. 42) that one night, in June 2012, he and two other witnesses (unnamed) saw an orange light, approximately the size of a double-decker bus, slowly descend and then hover over the camp. It moved against the direction of a strong breeze blowing from the south-west, and there was no flickering. Therefore, it didn't appear to be a Chinese lantern. It suddenly vanished.

On p. 50, Hennessey refers to a supposed sighting of an alien-like being in a silver suit near the camp. However, he doesn't say whether he spoke to, or corresponded with, the unnamed witness or witnesses. Indeed, he's generally rather vague in his reporting about the local phenomena.

Hennessey refers to a John (or 'Jackie') Gillies, who lives in a southern part of Gorebridge known as Birkenside. He has reportedly been filming strange aerial phenomena in the area since around 1999 (p. 47). In the article referenced in Note 4, Hennessey mentions various strange experiences reported by Gillies. For example, on a night in 2008, Gillies looked out of a window of his home and reportedly saw what appeared to be a blue strobing light. At first, he assumed that a police or fire-service vehicle was outside, which wasn't the case. Then, it seemed that the blue lights were *inside* the house. Hennessey notes that this wasn't an isolated incident: since the beginning of that year, the Gillies family had been woken almost every night, between 3.30 and 4 a.m., by a noise or some other disturbance. Several of their neighbours had been similarly affected. More extraordinarily, the article mentions an occasion when Gillies was at Middleton and allegedly saw a 'portal' open up, and then witnessed massive space ships offloading supplies. While that was going on, he was supposedly able to peer through space and observe plains and cities on Mars! Of course, critics might suggest that at least some of these experiences were purely subjective.

According to Hennessey's book, in the early morning of 3 December 2007, an unnamed female driver and an unnamed male driver reportedly had a UFO close encounter on the B704 road near Dalhousie Castle. They were heading north-west, and were at traffic lights just before the bridge over the River South Esk. The incident included classic features, such as their car engines and lights temporarily failing, and possible 'alien abduction' (p. 32; pp. 54–57). I don't know whether any investigator managed to obtain first-hand testimony from the male driver (assuming that he existed). As for the female, Hennessey states, in an internet article, that her husband purports to be 'an alien Fleet commander' who can make space ships appear at will and then film them, and that he's linked with 'Greys', who utilise an extensive cavern system in the general area![5,6] Of course, without hard corroborating evidence, such dramatic assertions could be seen as diminishing the credibility of the woman's UFO report.

Hennessey states that the fields between Dalhousie Castle and Carrington (a hamlet approximately 2 miles west-south-west of Gorebridge) have been reported to light up at night (p. 50), and that strange UFO phenomena are currently being witnessed between Gorebridge and the village of Middleton (p. 166). But regarding the latter, he may be referring to *North* Middleton rather than to Middleton itself, which is more of a hamlet than a village. North Middleton is about 2 miles south-south-east of Gorebridge.

Hennessey's book contains various photographs or video captures of supposed UFOs and other manifestations. However, to my mind, they're generally very unclear. On p. 44, for instance, there's one that purportedly depicts an alien 'Grey' seen near Gorebridge. But in my view, that interpretation is fanciful, because the image is very amorphous.

The imposing ruin of Crichton Castle is located a couple of miles east of Gorebridge, at the head of the River Tyne. It's a scheduled ancient monument, administered by Historic Scotland. According to the article referenced in Note 4, Hennessey has obtained pictures of 'Greys' in the woods nearby, along with close photos of some 'unknown technological artifact'.

PERSONAL INVESTIGATION AND ENQUIRIES

If the Gorebridge area is indeed hosting so much strange activity, I would have expected the phenomena to be the 'talk of the town'. In July 2017, I wrote to Andrew Bathgate, a board member of the Gorebridge Community Development Trust (GCDT), asking whether, to his knowledge, anomalous phenomena were being experienced in and around the village. I received no reply. Two subsequent emails to the GCDT seemed to fall on deaf ears. But then, weeks later, Linda Melrose, GCDT's administrator and bookkeeper, informed me that: 'Unfortunately, the members of GCDT have no knowledge or expertise in this matter, [and] therefore they are unable to assist you with this query.'

At the beginning of September 2017, I had a short telephone conversation with a reporter from the *Midlothian Advertiser*. He told me that he'd been covering the Gorebridge area for five years. In that time, he'd heard of only two incidents, although nothing came of them. He mentioned that Gorebridge lies under the flight path of Edinburgh Airport. However, since the airport is about 14 miles away, I doubt whether aircraft would be at a sufficiently low altitude over Gorebridge to account for the light phenomena mentioned by Hennessey. Regarding the camp, the reporter said something about people going there at night for the purpose of 'dogging' (meeting others for casual sex). I don't know whether that was conjecture or a joke, or whether the camp is indeed a place where 'dogging' occurs. If it is, maybe the flashing of car headlights has sometimes been mistaken for UFO activity.

During a daytime visit to Gorebridge in July 2017, I walked up to the camp from Gorebridge. I spoke to a man who appeared to be engaged in some sort of work (looking after livestock, perhaps). But he didn't seem to know about any strange phenomena there. Certainly, to me, the place didn't give any 'odd vibes', and I encountered no UFOs or aliens! During a further daytime visit, in early September 2017, I parked my car at the north-eastern end of Camp Wood and had an uneventful walk through it and back. I then spoke to a dog-walker on the lane where I'd parked my car. Although local to the area, she didn't appear to be aware of any reports of anomalous phenomena. An enquiry at Gorebridge library that day also drew a blank. The staff member I spoke to was aware that Andrew Hennessey had made claims about the area, but she said that the library had nothing by anyone else concerning such things. She mentioned that someone had supposedly seen a red light in the sky at 'Grange' (Newtongrange, presumably). But apart from that, she appeared to be unaware of any reports of strange activity in the locality.

During a night-time visit to the area in late September 2018, I witnessed nothing remarkable. That doesn't, of course, entitle me to infer that strange lights and other phenomena have never been witnessed there at night. But if the locality is as 'active' as Hennessey portrays it to be, I would have expected there to be more named witnesses.

COMMENTS

In Andrew Hennessey's view, aliens are responsible for the mysterious lights that he and others have reportedly seen in the area. Another possibility is that the locality is prone to natural phenomena known as *earth lights*. However, before delving into this matter, I'll make a short detour to mention the connection between light phenomena and earthquakes.

THE TECTONIC STRAIN THEORY

Michael Persinger (1945–2018), an American neuropsychologist, suggested that energy effects associated with tectonic strain could play a role in anomalous phenomena. His *tectonic strain theory* (TST) has been the subject of much discussion. A 1999 article by him, available on the internet, gives a flavour of his theorising, although it's couched in rather dense technical jargon, and it contains some faulty syntax.[7]

The tectonic plates that make up the Earth's crust slowly move on top of the magma (molten rock) below. Where the plates collide or grind past one another, or where there's movement along fractures (faults) elsewhere, earthquakes occur. It's recognised that lights are sometimes seen just before, during or after major earthquakes. They've been dubbed *earthquake lights*. But Persinger argued that light phenomena can also occur when geological stresses are building up, perhaps even months or years before an actual earthquake. He contended that witnesses might interpret them as UFOs. He also argued that variations in local stresses often follow earthquakes, and therefore UFOs may be seen then, although not as often as when stress is accumulating.

According to the TST, the lights, which are typically spherical or elliptical, will be seen in geologically faulted areas. They will tend to be seen near sharp features that concentrate electric charge (cliffs, towers, etc.) or near sources of electric charge (e.g. high-tension power lines), and they might move along fault lines. Depending on the characteristics of the fault and the local stress-field, they might make sudden right-angle turns, display quick or slow movements, or make sudden diving movements – which witnesses could misinterpret as evidence of intelligent control. The lights might be attracted to insulated charged objects, such as moving cars. Where strain has accumulated in the crustal rock, natural events or human activity (e.g. severe windstorms or the filling of reservoirs) might precipitate light phenomena. Lights might flash or blink in accordance with changes in the electric field involved, and witnesses might misinterpret this in terms of signalling, or think that the UFO has disappeared and then reappeared. If witnesses come into contact with the luminosities, the energy could affect them. For example, stimulation of certain parts of the brain could result in their hearing voices, seeing figures or experiencing amnesia.

EARTH LIGHTS

Areas such as Norway's Hessdalen valley and England's Longdendale have been the setting for recurrent sightings of unusual lights.[8] Paul Devereux, a British researcher, refers to them as *earth lights*. According to his website, they're natural phenomena that appear to be related to earthquake lights and ball lightning, but which have distinctive characteristics of their own.[9] For example, they sometimes last longer than earthquake lights and ball lightning. Devereux believes that they're associated with stresses and strains in the Earth's crust, but they can occur in the absence of actual earthquakes, and that they have electrical and magnetic properties. He states that 'some form of plasma is assumed', and that witnesses who come close to earth lights typically report hallucinatory experiences. He notes that earth lights sometimes behave as if they had a rudimentary intelligence. Another observation is that they sometimes manifest illogical effects, such as being visible from one side but not the other. Devereux infers from this that they may be what he calls 'macro-quantal events' – 'phenomena that should only exist at the sub-atomic quantum level, but [which somehow manifest] on our larger macro-scale of experience.'

In 1904 and 1905, there was a wave of sightings of strange lights along the Welsh coast between Barmouth and Harlech.[10] Light phenomena were also witnessed there in 1693 and 1694. At the time of the 1904/5 sightings, the lights were construed as divine manifestations associated with the Welsh religious revival and a local preacher, Mrs Mary Jones. Indeed, many of the sightings occurred around Egryn Chapel, where she preached. Interestingly, though, the area is home to significant geological faulting, and there'd been earthquake activity there in 1903. An article by Paul Devereux, Paul McCartney and Don Robins notes that all of the reliably positioned events occurred within 500 metres of a fault – usually the Mochras Fault.[11] They point out that Egryn Chapel is less than 100m from it, and that a chapel at Llanfair (where lights were also seen) is actually located on the fault.

However, if there's a tricksterish intelligence behind many anomalous phenomena, it's possible that it deliberately stages manifestations in such a way as to generate uncertainty about whether they were truly paranormal. Orchestrating phenomena in geologically faulted areas could be one way of doing that!

GEOLOGICAL FAULTING IN THE GOREBRIDGE AREA

In August 2018, I contacted the British Geological Survey (BGS), asking whether there's any significant geological faulting in or around Gorebridge. One of their scientific staff replied, stating that there are multiple faults in the area, and explaining that:

> Although in general they are considered inactive (or 'fossilised') faults, every now and again (and we are talking of geological-scale time) they may very slightly re-activate, causing micro-tremors. Still, these micro-tremors are unlikely to cause any worries to us, humans, or damage to our properties.

That may be so, but evidence indicates that mining operations in geologically faulted localities can activate faults and lead to ground disturbance and damage to buildings.[12]

The information I received from the BGS representative indicates that there are geological faults in the vicinity of Camp Wood. As noted above, Andrew Hennessey and others have reportedly seen strange lights thereabouts. However, there are many faulted areas in Scotland that *don't* seem to be associated with strange light manifestations, and I can't say for certain that the lights mentioned by Hennessey were produced by geological mechanisms.

4

STRANGE SIGHTINGS IN CORNWALL

Over the years, there've been numerous sightings of strange animals or animal-like creatures throughout Britain. Broadly speaking, the entities fall into two main categories: *out-of-place animals* and *quasi-animals*. The 'out-of-place' category includes, for example, sightings of big cats. Many examples are cited in Merrily Harpur's interesting book *Mystery Big Cats*. However, there's debate about whether such sightings are generated by actual flesh-and-blood creatures. Harpur believes that these experiences often have a paranormal aspect.

The second category, that of 'quasi-animals', entails sightings of entities, such as mermaids and werewolves, that have no recognised existence in official zoology. This chapter discusses a quasi-animal case from southern Cornwall, in the far southwest of England. It involved alleged sightings of a large owl-like creature that looked in some respects like a human. But before delving into the case, I'd like to refer more generally to anomalous experiences involving owls or owl-like entities.

OWLS AND THE PARANORMAL

Mike Clelland, a US-based outdoorsman and illustrator, has written an interesting and wide-ranging book entitled *The Messengers: Owls, Synchronicity and the UFO Abductee*. He describes intriguing personal experiences, and also relates numerous stories from other witnesses. The following are a few examples. The page numbers relate to his book.

In the autumn of 2006, Clelland and a friend, Kristen, had an unusual experience while spending a night out camping in the mountains near Clelland's then home (pp. 12–14). They spoke of their spiritual beliefs and insights, and there came a point in the conversation where Clelland felt a strong and 'hugely life affirming' connection with Kristen. Just then, an owl swooped over them, only a few feet above their heads. A second one appeared, and then a third. The owls circled and swooped silently over the couple for more than an hour. (Nearly three years later, Clelland asked Kristen whether she recalled what they'd been talking about when the first owl appeared. She said that she'd been trying to articulate her deepest beliefs about God.) They went camping again less than a week later, in a different part of the mountains. Three owls appeared and flew around them. After perching on nearby branches, they eventually landed on the ground and stared at the couple, within a few yards of them.

An informant called Cynthia, whom Clelland describes as having had experiences suggestive of alien abduction, was driving at night in Los Angeles with a friend. Their conversation turned to the subject of God. Right then, an owl swooped low across their field of view, frighteningly close to the vehicle's windscreen. Cynthia observed that the clock read 11:11. Clelland notes that this number has a curious way of showing up in connection with odd events (p. 93).

A woman told Clelland about an occasion when she set out to kill herself after years of depression (p. 301). She was driving towards the place of her intended suicide when she saw a large, snowy white owl. It appeared out of the darkness and flew towards her. She stopped, and the owl hovered within a foot of her windscreen for ten seconds or so, staring at her. She sensed that she was being told to be patient, and that her life would get better. Consequently, she decided not to kill herself.

It has been suggested that aliens are able to influence the minds of people they abduct, substituting more palatable, conventional imagery (e.g. of deer or owls) for what would otherwise be traumatic recollections of the abductors. These supposedly false recollections have been referred to as 'screen memories'. Clelland uses this expression, but in a way that applies not only to an abductee's recollections, but also to what was experienced during the supposed abduction itself. Arguably, though, if abductees misperceive their abductors as non-alien creatures such as owls, it would be better to describe their false perceptions as screen *images*, not memories.

Clelland concedes that not all anomalous sightings of owls are what they seem, but he thinks that real owls are involved in some cases. If so, it would seem that these birds are sometimes taken over by an external intelligence, which uses them as 'messengers' or symbols, perhaps because they already have a well-established place in mythology.

Although Clelland doesn't seem firmly attached to any particular theory, he evidently believes that there are spiritual and paranormal forces at work in our lives, and that anomalous owl experiences can serve as important messages or signs. Overall, he appears to construe paranormal and UFO-related phenomena in a positive light. Even in the case of alien abduction experiences, he appears inclined to attribute good intentions to the presumed intelligence(s) behind the phenomena. Indeed, he's concluded that UFO abduction 'is a spiritual path' (p. 97), although he acknowledges that it can be traumatic for abductees. However, many people would regard this stance as naively positive, and it appears that the majority of the people who report alien-abduction experiences find them distressing, not spiritually uplifting.

THE OWLMAN OF MAWNAN

Jonathan Downes heads a Devon-based organisation called the Centre for Fortean Zoology (CFZ). It carries out research in the UK and overseas regarding animals whose existence isn't officially recognised, and it publishes books under the banner 'CFZ Press'. The adjective 'Fortean' in CFZ's name reflects the fact that the organisation takes an interest in paranormal manifestations featuring animal-like entities. The word is derived from the surname of Charles Hoy Fort (1874 –1932), an American writer who compiled reports of strange phenomena.

A book by Downes, titled *The Owlman and Others*, discusses a series of *alleged* sightings of a strange owl-like entity (referred to as the 'Owlman') in Cornwall between 1976 and 1995. It was first published in 1997. I've emphasised the word 'alleged' because there's uncertainty about the reliability of some of the stories. In citing page numbers, I'll be referring to the 2006 edition of the book. The Owlman sightings are the prime focus of the book, but Downes has presented them in a rather disjointed way, interspersed with other material, and it's not possible to see, at a glance, how many sightings there were. Indeed, I don't know whether Downes has mentioned every alleged sighting that he's aware of. At any rate, I get the impression that the total number was small, perhaps not even reaching double figures.

THE ROLE OF TONY SHIELS

A man named Tony Shiels features prominently in Downes' book. He's also known as 'Doc' Shiels but, as far as I know, he doesn't have a doctoral degree. He was born in Salford in 1938, apparently of Scottish and Irish descent. He lived in Cornwall for many years, but is now based in Ireland. He's an artist and writer. In Cornwall, he rediscovered stage magic, which he'd been taught as a boy, and he performed as the 'Wizard of the West'. He put on theatrical performances with members of his large family and attracted publicity via 'monster-raising' exploits, some of which involved naked female witches. In 1977, he supposedly obtained photos of the Loch Ness Monster. He regards himself, first and foremost, as an artist; and he considers his life's work to be a form of surrealism that he describes as 'surrealchemy'. (Surrealism is a movement in art and literature that aims at giving expression to the unconscious mind.)

Judging from his book, Downes believes that Shiels has exhibited genuine psychic powers (p. 57), and that he's probably the wisest and most powerful man that he (Downes) has ever met (p. 249)! But Shiels appears to have been something of a trickster. Downes refers to an occasion when Shiels planned to fabricate a photograph of UFOs (p. 121); and in the Introduction to Downes' book, Shiels describes himself as a 'shameless mountebank' and 'teller of truthful lies' (p. 15). Therefore, there are grounds for being cautious in evaluating the stories about strange events that he's conveyed. Indeed, in discussing one of the alleged sightings of the mysterious winged entity that came to be known as the Owlman, Downes refers to inconsistencies in what Shiels told different people (pp. 49–51).

THE LOCATION

Leaving aside a rumoured sighting near Lamorna, some miles to the west (see below), it seems that most, if not all, of the alleged appearances were in the immediate vicinity of the Church of St Mawnan and St Stephen. I say 'most, if not all' because one of the witnesses, Gavin (see below), wasn't absolutely certain that he could remember the church, which Downes refers to as 'Mawnan Old Church'. I'll refer to it simply as 'Mawnan church'. Mawnan, where the church is located, consists of a scattering of properties, probably mainly farm premises, and could be better described as a hamlet than a village. The village of Mawnan Smith is less than a mile to the north-west.

Mawnan church. (W.J. Hoyland)

The graveyard. (W.J. Hoyland)

Mawnan church is abutted by woodland on its western, northern and eastern sides. To its south, there's a graveyard and then more woodland. Part of the South West Coast Path runs through the latter. Further south, beyond these woods, there's the estuary of the River Helford.

SIGHTINGS

For ease of expression, I'll be sparing in the use of 'distancing terminology' ('alleged', 'reported', etc.). The evidential status of the individual reports might be deemed weak. But, taken together, they do perhaps suggest that something unusual was going on. The following are details of some of them. The cited page numbers relate to Downes' book.

The first incident supposedly occurred on Easter Saturday in 1976. It involved a family of four: Don Melling, his wife and their two daughters.[1] They were on holiday in Cornwall and stopped for a picnic lunch in the woods next to Mawnan church. Twelve-year-old June and her 9-year-old sister, Vicky, went off to play among the gravestones while their parents set about preparing the lunch. But then, presumably only a short time later, the girls screamed in terror and ran back to the car, panic-stricken. They wanted to be taken home as quickly as possible. The family returned to their 'caravan site' or 'campsite' (Downes, p. 24, is inconsistent regarding this detail), where the girls explained what had happened: they'd apparently heard an odd noise and seen a huge, feathered 'bird-man' hovering over the church tower. Later that day, at Penryn Steam Fair, Tony Shiels was pointed out to Don Melling, with the suggestion that he (Shiels) was responsible for all of the mysterious goings-on in that part of the county. Melling spoke to him, apparently thinking that it was a prank by Shiels that had frightened the girls. Shiels assured Melling that he'd done nothing of the sort, and he asked to speak to the children. Melling refused, but reportedly gave Shiels a drawing, made by June, depicting the flying entity. A letter from Shiels, describing the incident, was subsequently published in the magazine *Fortean Times*. An illustration, based on June's drawing, appeared beneath it.

This story about the Melling family hasn't been corroborated. Downes considers the possibility that it was invented by Shiels, but he seems to give his old friend the benefit of the doubt (p. 244). However, in a video, available on YouTube, Downes told Dr Darren Naish that some of the Owlman accounts were hoaxes by people he knew, and he thought that Shiels had invented the Owlman for fun.[2] But then, 'when it started to come true, no one was more surprised than [Shiels].' Downes added that

Shiels hadn't quite admitted this to him, but he hadn't told him he was wrong. It's not clear from the documentary whether the story about June and Vicky Melling is one of those that Downes regards as bogus. But if it's the first tale in a saga that began as pure invention, it's presumably a fabrication.

According to an unsubstantiated rumour heard by Shiels, the entity was seen again, around 11 May 1976, near Lamorna, a village a few miles south of Penzance, in the far west of Cornwall (pp. 32–33).

Around 10 p.m. on 3 July 1976, two 14-year-old girls, who were camping near Mawnan church, heard a strange hissing noise nearby and then saw the creature standing no more than 20 yards away. It flew up, disappearing in the trees. Shiels claimed that he learned of this incident the next day, having encountered the girls on the beach below the church. In the summer of 2000, Downes received a long email (reproduced on p. 34 and pp. 39–40 of his book) from a 'Sally G', who purported to have been one of the witnesses. She explained that an acquaintance of hers had found Downes on the internet and had suggested that she write to him. She described the incident in some detail, correcting one or two minor points in the version related by Shiels. But without corroboration, it's impossible to be sure whether the account is genuine. Judging from the book, she simply gave her address as 'Pembroke, Wales'; and it seems that she refrained from giving her then surname (unless, of course, Downes has withheld it).

In 1995, Downes and a colleague made contact with a man of about 20. He seems to have been the only Owlman witness that Downes actually got to meet. The book gives him the pseudonym 'Gavin'. Downes is confident that there'd been no collusion between Shiels and this witness. Gavin believed that his experience had probably occurred in the summer of 1988 or 1989. At the time, he'd been on holiday with his then girlfriend and her parents. The sighting occurred one evening when he was out for a walk with his female friend. He couldn't recall precisely where they were – he thought that he could remember the church, but he wasn't absolutely sure. At any rate, the beam of his torch illuminated a creature that was standing on the branch of a tree, about 15 feet above the ground. It was about 4 or 4½ feet tall. Its torso was like that of a man, but had a texture resembling soft bird feathers. Its feet were black and pincer-like. The face was flat, with its black mouth curving down sharply. The creature's arms or wings were quite large, and were held out at the sides, with long, light-grey feathers – the same colour as the rest of its body. After retracting its arms or wings, the creature jumped down behind the tree. Following a momentary pause, Gavin and his friend fled.

Someone claiming to be a female American student wrote to the *Western Morning News* in 1995, describing a very recent Owlman sighting near the church. Downes wrote to this supposed witness, but received no reply.

INDEPENDENT TESTIMONY

A Facebook contact has given me some interesting information. In the 1990s, when her name was Barbara Fennell, she set up a paranormal investigation group in London. One of the members, Alan, had grown up in Mullion, in southern Cornwall. He said that he knew someone who'd seen the Owlman, and that he would enquire whether she was still around. He discovered that she was living in Penzance. In July 1998, in the course of a visit to Cornwall, Barbara and members of her group met the 32-year-old witness, whom I'll call Kate, which isn't her real name. Barbara felt that Kate's testimony was sincere. Her story is very similar to those contained in Downes' book and lends support to the argument that at least some of the supposed incidents truly occurred. The following is a statement that Kate gave to Barbara and her group. I've edited it for presentational purposes, but I haven't changed the substantive content:

One evening in late May 1978, when I was 12 years old, I was playing on the road beside Mawnan church. It was early dusk. I was late for tea, so I ran towards my home. I was with my friend Ann [pseudonym]. As we neared the church, Ann slowed down and suddenly started looking over towards the side of the building. I carried on, but Ann screamed at me, and then caught up with me, grabbing my arm. I was about to tell her to let go, and say we should go home, but she started crying and pointing towards the church. I thought she was larking about, but I could see that she was very scared. She said that she'd seen a huge man with wings. I laughed and told her to shut up. But I was a bit scared. However, we were always larking about with each other, so I thought that it was a joke.

As Ann calmed down, I looked back, and saw a huge birdman-like creature starting to fly towards the farm. It was sort of rising after taking off. It seemed about four feet long and had a pointy beak and huge eyes. They weren't red or anything, but they were looking at us. Here's the thing, though: it had human-like features, such as a mouth and lips, but with a beak where the nose would be. The wings were the scariest part. They were almost like a huge feathery cloak, which seemed to move together as it flapped. They hardly seemed to separate, like a bird's wings do. Even to this day, I've never seen anything so bizarre as that. The feet were very crooked and pointed, but the 'legs' were solid up to the point where the feet met. It had very dark brown feathers, with silvery bits. It was truly frightening.

The whole atmosphere changed and went silent, except for the sound of its wings. I'd swear that as we cowered into the hedge, it was still looking at us. Then, it did a half-turn, and disappeared into the woods. I was so scared that I avoided being out at night and in the evening for many months after. After all these years, I can only say that I don't believe it was a bloody owl. I've seen plenty of them in flight, but this was too large and just plain strange. I'm not stupid, or blind, but no one believed me then, although there were rumours about it over a couple of years.

CONCURRENT WEIRDNESS

It appears that there was a lot of strange activity in southern Cornwall in 1976, the year in which the Owlman sightings were first reported. In fact, Downes' research suggested that the regional weirdness had apparently started towards the end of 1975 and had continued until around February or March of 1977 (p. 117). There were, for example, UFO sightings, mysterious bangs in the sky (some of which may have been sonic booms from Concorde flights), and mysterious disappearances of live-stock. Arguably, though, without comparative data from other regions, it's impossible to know for sure whether the area hosted a disproportionate number of strange occurrences. Even if it had, it wouldn't necessarily mean that there was a fundamental con-nection between the different types of event. It's conceivable, for instance, that there was no connection between the aerial bangs and the livestock disappearances.

'PSYCHIC BACKLASH'

Downes explains that while he was working on his book about the Owlman, bad luck befell him: two of his pet cats died sud-denly, two computers and two cars blew up, and his wife left him (pp. 9–10). He concedes that his marriage was rocky, and that his cats, computers and cars had seen better days. But he states that this sort of thing has plagued him repeatedly when he's been on the track of Owlman and the like. Shiels had apparently warned him about this (supposed) phenomenon of 'psychic backlash'.

However, it's commonplace for us to experience periods when things go badly. It's only to be expected that this will happen from time to time, purely by chance. Therefore, it's questionable whether there was anything psychic about the bad luck that Downes experienced.

EXPLANATIONS AND SPECULATIONS

One proffered explanation for the Owlman sightings is that the witnesses saw a real owl but overestimated its size. Downes rejects that theory. He notes, for example, that he's not aware of any records of 'aberrant owls' being seen elsewhere in southern Cornwall between 1976 and 1995 (p. 232). (But, as indicated above, there was a rumoured sighting near Lamorna.) Downes considers it significant that all of the sightings involved young female witnesses (p. 232). (Gavin seems to have been the only male witness, although he was in the company of a girl of about 13 when he allegedly saw the entity.)

Downes contends that Tony Shiels would have been capable of making up the whole thing. But largely because of Gavin's testimony, Downes rejects that possibility. Instead, he interprets the Owlman sightings in paranormal terms, although he doesn't articulate a clear theory.

Downes reports that Shiels had repeatedly urged him to learn about surrealism. Shiels contended that it was important to understanding the Owlman phenomenon. Then Shiels phoned, telling him to learn more about the German surrealist painter

Max Ernst (1891–1976). Ernst had visited Cornwall in 1937. Interestingly, but perhaps merely coincidentally, he died on 1 April 1976, about two weeks before the first alleged Owlman sighting. Furthermore, a recurrent image in Ernst's paintings was that of a human figure with a bird-like head.

It might be conjectured that the Owlman sightings were paranormal displays that mimicked Ernst's art. On the other hand, if most of the reports are deemed to have been mischievous inventions by Shiels, this resonance with Ernst's work could be put down to the fact that Shiels was familiar with Ernst's art. However, if Downes is right in thinking that there'd been no collusion between Shiels and Gavin, it's hard to explain away the latter's testimony, unless we assume that Gavin was a prankster operating independently. Also, of course, we have the witness referred to above as Kate, whose testimony didn't come via Tony Shiels.

The Owlman sightings induced fear in the witnesses. But could that have been intended, to deter girls and young women from placing themselves in danger? Take, for example, the above-mentioned case of two 14-year-old girls who allegedly saw the entity while camping in the woods near Mawnan church. Assuming that the story is true, it could be argued that the girls were putting themselves at risk by being there alone at night. Paradoxically, they might have been safer camping in a much more remote location, well away from the possible attention of would-be attackers.

I'm not aware of any reports of child molestation and the like from the immediate vicinity of Mawnan, but there have been cases from the wider area. A *Mail Online* article from 2012 refers to the conviction of two elderly men who'd been charged with a string of sexual offences against children in Cornwall, stretching back to the 1970s.[3] They are said to have been members of a pagan group.

5

THE
'FIFE INCIDENT'

Fife is one of the thirty-two single-tier council areas in modern-day Scotland. It was formerly classed as a county. Located in east-central Scotland, it's geographically a peninsula that projects eastwards into the North Sea. It lies north of Edinburgh and the Firth of Forth, and south of Dundee and the Firth of Tay. To the west, it has land boundaries with two other council areas: Perth and Kinross, and Clackmannanshire. The highest point in Fife is a hill known as the West Lomond (522m/1,713ft).

The main events of the case discussed in this chapter supposedly occurred on the evening of 23 September 1996, possibly extending into the very early part of the 24th. They happened in the vicinity of Newton of Falkland, a hamlet near Falkland Hill (also known as the East Lomond), which rises to over 1,400 feet and is the second highest point in Fife. The case is known as the 'Fife Incident', which is a misnomer, because there were multiple incidents, albeit squeezed into a narrow time frame.

SOURCES

A website by someone using the name 'Jayess' (possibly a phonetic rendering of the initials 'J.S.') is helpful, because it reproduces a lot of source material bearing on the case.[1] It also provides some critical commentary. However, 'Jayess' doesn't identify him- or herself, and the title used ('The Falkland Hill Incident') is inaccurate, since the principal events *didn't* occur on Falkland Hill.

Malcolm Robinson, head of a group called Strange Phenomena Investigations (SPI), discusses the case at considerable length in Volume 1 of his book *UFO Case Files of Scotland* (pp. 241–354). It's also covered, albeit more briefly, by Ron Halliday in his book *UFO Scotland* (pp. 160–64). In an internet article, Marcus Lowth presents a summary of the case, but gets some of the details wrong.[2] The late Tony Dodd became aware of the case at an early stage and discussed it in his book *Alien Investigator* (pp. 84–88). But he didn't have any face-to-face contact with the witnesses, and his portrayal of the events was also flawed.

CONFUSION OVER THE LOCATION

Unfortunately, there's been some confusion over the location. In a 1997 article headed 'Statement on the Fife Incident!', which is available on the Jayess website, Malcolm Robinson admitted that he 'lied to many press agencies' when he was urged to reveal where the events had occurred. He falsely claimed that it was near Kennoway, Fife. (Henceforth, I'll refer to this article as his 'Incident Statement'.) In a 2003 article, he explained that having guaranteed the witnesses anonymity, he gave the wrong location to ensure that no one from the press would be able to find them by 'snooping' in the relevant area.[3] But instead of lying

Newton of Falkland.

about it, he could have simply refrained from naming the place. After all, deceiving the media is tantamount to lying to the wider public. Author and researcher Ron Halliday, for one, may have been misled by this disinformation, because his book states that the events happened 'close to Kennoway' (p. 160). In any case, I doubt whether the anonymity of the witnesses would have been compromised if the true location had been revealed at the outset. Certainly, it's impossible to evaluate a UFO case properly without knowing the location.

OUTLINE OF THE EVENTS

Various investigators looked into the case, not only Tony Dodd and Malcolm Robinson. There were four witnesses, whom Dodd refers to as Mary, Peter, Jane and Susan. But these are apparently pseudonyms. Mary and Jane were in their 30s at the time. Peter was Mary's 10-year-old son; and Susan, nearly 15, was Jane's daughter. On the evening of 23 September 1996, Mary and Peter visited Jane's home in, or near, the picturesque village of Falkland, Fife.

Below, I've given a brief outline of the events, drawing principally on a statement from Mary ('The Falkland Hill landing: the true story'), available on the Jayess website. At points, though, her testimony is confusing, since it's not clear exactly where she and her companions were supposed to have been, and in what direction they were looking.

The witnesses' experiences can be divided into five phases. It would have been helpful to have detailed maps relating to Phases 3 and 4.

PHASE 1: THE JOURNEY TO FREUCHIE

At 7.30 p.m. on the evening in question, Mary, Peter and Jane set out on a short drive to buy some coffee and cigarettes at a shop in Freuchie, a village approximately 2 miles east (and slightly south) of Falkland. Mary did the driving. Their route along the B936 road took them through the hamlet of Newton of Falkland. As they were approaching or leaving the hamlet – Mary's testimony is inconsistent regarding this[4] – they had a UFO experience, beginning with her spotting 'a huge, horizontally oval, brilliantly white light … low in the sky'. When she looked at it a third time, it had changed to two circular lights, like massive, stationary headlamps. She drew Jane's attention to them. They were visible above, and beyond, a farmhouse (Newton of Lathrisk, I presume) to the left of the road. The lights changed their orientation, directing massive beams down to the field below. A craft could be seen in silhouette. Mary stopped the car at a gap between a wall and a hedge bordering the road. They watched the object for a few moments. It then switched off its lights and began to move slowly, making no noise. Mary got out of her car. She looked up at the underside of the UFO, which was triangular. A small red light came on at each apex, followed by two more at each apex, making nine lights in all. Mary got back into the car. All three of the witnesses then got out to look at the receding UFO. It seemed to be aware of them. For example, when Mary flashed her car's headlights, it flashed back.

PHASE 2: THE JOURNEY BACK FROM FREUCHIE

As they were leaving Freuchie, the witnesses saw the UFO again (or possibly a different one) moving rapidly, on a parallel course. It then turned and approached them at high speed. Mary stopped the car, and the craft began to switch on lots of lights. Peter screamed. Mary turned, to try to reach and comfort him. The UFO extinguished its lights and jumped back into the distance.

In Jane's home village (Falkland, I presume), they looked through a UFO magazine that they'd bought in the village store in Freuchie. They found a telephone number for a UFO investigation group called Skysearch and rang it from a public phone box. After leaving a recorded message about their UFO sightings, they returned to Jane's home. Her daughter, Susan, said that they'd been away for over an hour, and they later concluded that they couldn't account for about fifteen minutes of the outward journey.

PHASE 3: A FURTHER EXCURSION

Impelled by curiosity, all four of them set out in Mary's car at 9.45 p.m. They stopped just to the east of Newton of Falkland. Across a field to their left, at the edge of some woods, there was a large bright white light. Shortly after, Mary noticed a blue glow to its left, shining up from the ground and through some trees.

They decided to proceed to the next village (Freuchie, presumably) and take a 'back lane', to get a better look. But in retrospect, it was apparent to them that that route wouldn't have taken them closer to where they'd seen the bright light and blue glow. However, as they were driving down the back lane, they noticed a 'star' on the ground, near some trees. (The precise location isn't specified.) Mary stopped the car, but left the engine running and the lights on, to facilitate a quick getaway, if required. The 'star' seemed to pulse with light; then it started shooting huge laser-like beams into the sky. The witnesses' felt strangely moved by the spectacle. Then, a figure moved from the right and stood in front of white light coming from the 'star'. From its silhouette, the figure seemed decidedly non-human. For example, it was slender, long-limbed, and had a disproportionately large head. It was joined by four or five other beings who were similarly shaped, but much smaller. After seemingly watching the witnesses for a few moments, the figures moved about, coming into and going out of sight. To the right of this spectacle, across a field behind a hedge and some small trees, there was a smaller version of the blue glow spotted earlier. (Again, it's not clear to me precisely where this was supposed to have been.) The blue glow outlined a black, structured shape on the ground. The witnesses noticed silhouetted 'beings' walking towards and behind it.

At that point, many more of the 'stars' appeared in the sky around the witnesses, and the road in front of their car was illuminated by a beam of light. Feeling scared, they decided to leave. Mary drove on until she reached a wide junction, where she was able to turn the car around and head back the way they'd come.

At some point, the others asked her to stop. She halted just before a humpback bridge, which I presume was a bridge over the

River Eden, about a mile north of Freuchie. To the left, in some woods, another 'star' and blue glow could be seen. But when Mary subsequently reported this to Tony Dodd, she found that her recollection was somewhat hazy and confused. After watching this latest spectacle for a short time, the witnesses returned to Jane's village, from where they phoned Skysearch again. This time, they managed to speak to Larry Dean of the group, who asked whether they had a video-camera, camera or binoculars. They had none of those, but they said that they would go back to the area and watch from a safe distance. However, they first returned to Jane's home, because her brother was due to call in for a coffee on his way home from work. He offered to lend them his binoculars.

PHASE 4: THE LAST EXCURSION

The four witnesses drove to the village where Jane's brother lived and collected the binoculars. Unfortunately, the village isn't named in Mary's accounts, and I don't know what route they took. However, in one of her statements, she said that going along the 'same road', she and her companions saw the first 'star' and blue glow were where they'd initially seen them. This may be a reference to the road going through Newton of Falkland (the B936). At any rate, keeping to main roads,[5] they were followed by lots of large, bright, white lights, low in the sky, and while approaching the village where Jane's brother lived, Mary saw a very large white light on the hill behind it, which started flashing – in a pattern of three flashes, then a pause, and then three more flashes.

It seems that after collecting the binoculars, the witnesses drove to the spot, just east of Newton of Falkland, where they'd parked previously.[6] Jane focused the binoculars on the 'star' (in, or near, the woods to the north, I presume). When Mary was eventually handed the binoculars and focused on the 'star', she heard two bursts of a buzzing, crackling type of noise to her left (which may have come from nearby power lines). She could see an object a couple of feet above the ground, revolving on a slightly tilted axis. Among other things, she described it as shimmering and being sort of ball shaped, but slightly elongated towards its top and bottom. A little to its right, on the ground, there was a disc-shaped object of a dull red colour, and further to the right she noticed the profile of a tall entity. To the left of all of this she could see a blue glow and an opening in the trees to a clearer area, where there was the outline of a large black structure and a lot of activity (e.g. entities carrying boxes and cylindrical containers).

Jane tended to 'hog' the binoculars. But Mary came to realise that she (Mary) could see the entities without them; and it seems that Susan and Peter were also able to make out more than one would have expected. This, along with other aspects of what's described, suggests that they may have been having visionary experiences (albeit perhaps paranormal) and not actually seeing objectively real events.

Eventually, Jane began saying that a mist was approaching them from the trees. And Susan said that 'they' were coming. Mary's recollection was that Peter was also saying something. Jane reportedly went on to claim that hundreds of entities, contained in cocoon-like structures, were coming across the field towards them. However, Mary herself saw round, straw bales in the field, casting shadows. But as she looked on, there seemed to be more and more of them, and they were getting closer. Then Mary had some odd experiences, beginning with her vision going 'funny'. As Jane shouted, 'Get the f[***] out of here!', Mary began driving away, and the field behind them lit up in a gigantic blue flash.

PHASE 5: BACK AT JANE'S HOME

Mary and Peter remained at Jane's house that night, but the adults got little or no sleep. At one point, while Jane was at the kitchen sink, she screamed, and shortly after explained to Mary that she'd seen an alien at the window. However, I'm not sure whether this refers to a flashback of something she'd experienced in Mary's car near the end of Phase 4, or whether she actually saw an alien-looking figure at her kitchen window.

ADDITIONAL INFORMATION

JANE

Malcolm Robinson and his SPI colleagues didn't get to interview Jane. But in a handwritten account that Larry Dean obtained from her, she depicted the events as having been transformational for her. For example, she apparently felt that her purpose on Earth had a new meaning, and that she'd been chosen for some special reason to help abolish hurt and negative tendencies towards others.[7]

MARY AND PETER

Mary and Peter had a history of strange experiences. For example, when Mary was living in Cupar, Fife, some years before the 'Fife Incident', there was an occasion when she felt a malevolent presence.[8] She and Peter continued to experience odd phenomena after the 'Fife Incident'. For example, on 20 October 1996, Peter looked out of his bedroom window and allegedly saw a small free-floating, white being looking at him; and he had another sighting of the entity (or a similar one) in the bathroom later that same day.[9] Mary informed SPI that she believed that she and her family were sharing their home with the ghost of a dog. She mentioned an occasion when the family heard it. Their cat ran out of the kitchen wide-eyed, with its tail bristling. When Mary and her husband went into the kitchen, they heard the sound of something lapping at the cat's water dish, although nothing could be seen.[10]

SHARON COULL

Within weeks of the event, Sharon Coull, a Fife-based UFO researcher, became friends with Mary. They met for the first time in mid-October, at Sharon's home. Mary was accompanied by Peter and Jane. That very night, shortly after the visitors had left, Sharon had some strange experiences. Odd phenomena continued at her home, including electrical problems. For example, on an occasion when she was angry, three light bulbs blew, one after the other! Eventually, her family's car was 'written off' in an accident. That more or less marked the end of a run of bad luck. Sharon wondered whether it had been connected with the 'Fife Incident'.[11]

COMMENTS

Robinson's 'Incident Statement' explains that after concluding that this was an impressive case, he went on to develop strong reservations. He cites two reasons: (1) the witnesses failed to respond to a number of letters from him; and (2) prior to the alleged events, Mary had subscribed to some UFO publications; and she'd even bought a UFO magazine on the evening of

23 September 1996. As he notes, by being 'clued up' on the UFO subject, she would have known what UFOs and their associated entities were supposed to look like! He considers the possibility that the story had been fabricated 'to test the gullibility of UFO researchers or just to see how far [it] would go'.

The 'Incident Statement' was reproduced in a small-circulation, undated and now defunct magazine called *Haunted Scotland* (Issue 13, pp. 7–10). It appeared (around 1999, I would guess) under the title 'The Fife Incident – why I know [*sic*] believe this to be a hoax'. This implies that Robinson had come to believe that the story was definitely a hoax, unless we're to assume that it was the editor, not Robinson himself, who came up with the second part of the title. However, the article itself didn't sound quite so categorical. Anyway, a 2016 online newspaper article, marking the 20th anniversary of the 'Fife Incident', stated that Robinson remained convinced that the witnesses *had* experienced something other-worldly.[12]

Of course, there could be various reasons why the witnesses failed to respond to Robinson's letters. So I don't think too much can be drawn from that. Mary gave a credible explanation for why she bought a UFO magazine on the evening of 23 September: she and her companions had just had a dramatic UFO experience, and she wanted to know where it could be reported. On the other hand, a UFO magazine isn't, perhaps, the sort of item one would normally see on sale in a village convenience store.

One of Tony Dodd's colleagues, Scotland-based Brian Rooney, visited the 'scene of the encounter'. I presume that that's a reference to the wooded area about half a mile north of the B936 road at Newton of Falkland. (However, as I've explained, the witnesses reportedly observed UFO/alien activity at more than just one site thereabouts.) He photographed burn marks and semicircular impressions on the ground. Trees and bushes nearby were heavily coated with a white material, looking like a spider's web, as if they'd been blasted with it. Dodd commented that although there was no motor access within 200 yards of the scene, Rooney was convinced that a heavy vehicle had been there.[13]

The online newspaper article from 2016, referenced in Note 12, quoted 73-year-old Tam Wright. It described him as being Newton of Falkland's 'longest residing resident'. He suggested that the witnesses had mistaken a night-time pea-harvesting operation for something alien. If pea-harvesting did indeed occur there on the night in question, it might account for at least some of the physical features noticed by Rooney. However, Wright's theory doesn't seem sufficiently comprehensive to account for everything that the witnesses reportedly experienced.

Electricity power lines run past Newton of Falkland on its eastern side, crossing the B936 road. Mary seems to have parked in that area on three occasions during the evening of 23 September 1996. Could the witnesses have been affected by the magnetic fields associated with the power lines? It's conceivable that the fields induced hallucinations and memory distortions, or somehow catalysed a paranormal experience. However, the initial UFO experience began as Mary, Jane and Peter were approaching or leaving Newton of Falkland. If it began as they were approaching the hamlet from the west, it's unlikely that they were sufficiently close to the power lines at that point to be affected by the magnetic fields. If the sighting began as they were leaving the hamlet, it's hard to believe that they had yet had sufficient exposure to the fields to be significantly affected. (It's worth remembering that their UFO sighting began *before* Mary had actually brought the car to a halt near the power lines.) Furthermore, the witnesses' sightings of UFOs and alien-looking entities weren't confined to locations close to power lines.

The power lines.

If their story is genuine, the witnesses may have had a succession of collective paranormal experiences of a private and hallucinatory nature, as if they'd been pretty much sharing the same dream. If so, other people in the area might well have noticed nothing unusual. As already noted, aspects of the witnesses' experiences are certainly suggestive of something visionary. For example, near the end of Phase 4, Mary and Jane saw things differently. However, it would be wrong to take the events of 23/24 September in isolation. As noted above, Sharon Coull reported that after receiving a visit from three of the witnesses the following month, strange things, including electrical problems, occurred at her home over a period of time. Was that merely coincidental?

If the witnesses had been living in a completely different part of the country, they might well have experienced very similar phenomena there. In other words, the events may have been 'person-centred' and not intrinsically linked with the area around Newton of Falkland.

6

CANNOCK CHASE — AN ANOMALY HOT SPOT?

Cannock Chase is a 26-square-mile area of woodland and heath in Staffordshire, in the West Midlands region of England. Judging from reports, it may be a hot spot for anomalous phenomena. Lying north of the Birmingham conurbation and south-east of Stafford, it's part of what was once a large hunting ground created by William the Conqueror and known as the King's Forest of Cannock. The development of settlements in the Middle Ages led to the clearing of woodland, which gathered pace in the sixteenth century, when trees were destroyed to produce charcoal. Fortunately, there's still a scattering of oaks, which are most abundant in Brocton Coppice, in the north-western part of the Chase. But much of the woodland is now coniferous rather than broadleaf.

The 1:25,000 (2½in to 1 mile) OS Explorer Map no. 244 (*Cannock Chase & Chasewater*) depicts the locality, which is classed as an Area of Outstanding Natural Beauty, although it's close to towns and is intersected by numerous roads and tracks (not shown in the outline map displayed here). A railway line runs through the Chase, roughly parallel to the A460 road between Hednesford and Rugeley.

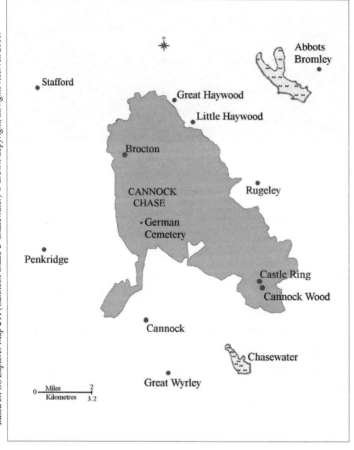

Based on OS Explorer Map 244 (Cannock Chase & Chasewater) © Crown Copyright, all rights reserved 2010.

Cannock Chase.

The German Military Cemetery.

Castle Ring, the site of an ancient hill fort, lies at the south-eastern end of Cannock Chase and marks its highest point (244m/801ft). It's next to the village of Cannock Wood, and has reportedly been the setting for strange phenomena. Some 4 miles to the north-west of Castle Ring, and within the Chase, are the Commonwealth Cemetery and the German Military Cemetery.[1] The latter, which is also known as the 'German War Cemetery' or simply the 'German Cemetery', was built in 1964 and inaugurated and dedicated in 1967. It contains the graves of nearly 5,000 Germans, Austrians and Ukrainians, many of whom had been servicemen during the two world wars. Under an agreement with the Federal Republic of Germany, their bodies were transferred to the cemetery from churchyards scattered about the country. Strange manifestations have reportedly occurred in its vicinity.

SOURCES

Nick Redfern, who was brought up in Pelsall, not far from Cannock Chase, is a prolific author of books and articles on UFO, cryptozoological and paranormal themes. He's been based in the United States for some years, but he's continued to take an interest in, and to publicise, accounts of strange phenomena on, and around, Cannock Chase. For example, the area receives attention in his books *Man-Monkey*, *There's Something in the Woods* and *The Monster Book*.

Cannock Chase.

Lee Brickley spent much of his childhood in Heath Hayes, close to Cannock Chase. His short book *UFOs, Werewolves & the Pig-Man* contains various interesting anecdotes about the locality. Other writers and researchers, such as Jenny Randles, have also referred to the area.

UFO SIGHTINGS

Cannock Chase has reportedly been the setting for UFO sightings. The following are a few examples, at least some of which may have purely prosaic explanations.

'FLYING TRIANGLES'

Numerous witnesses saw a couple of 'flying triangles' in the area on the evening of 16 May 1988, although according to David Clarke, a sceptical writer on UFO matters, they were two VC10 aircraft, from 101 Squadron, RAF Brize Norton, lining up for an in-flight refuelling exercise, which was to take place over the North Sea. He contends that flying very high and slowly, they were misinterpreted as low-level, silent objects that even seemed to hover.[2]

Some years ago, Omar Fowler, a Derby-based ufologist, sent me details of a sighting that reportedly occurred near the town of Rugeley one night in July 1997. That would have been close to, if not over, Cannock Chase. But Fowler (now deceased) believed that it may have involved a stealth aircraft rather than something exotic. The witness heard a noise outside his home, similar to that of a high-revving two-stroke engine. He went outside and saw lights hovering approximately 150 yards away and 150 feet above the ground. After going indoors to fetch binoculars, he was able to make out the shape of a black helicopter in the vicinity of the lights. He went back indoors and returned with a night vision scope. He could see the helicopter clearly, since it was illuminated by the flashing strobe and navigation lights. When he turned on the infrared beam, he saw a blacked-out triangular craft next to the helicopter. It was similar in size to the helicopter, but it reflected no light from the strobe and navigation lights. Looking through his night scope, the witness approached the two hovering craft. Suddenly, the helicopter shot away at an incredibly high speed. The triangle remained for a moment but then moved out of sight.

Something similar may have been witnessed in Greater Manchester the previous year. Fowler informed me that the 22 August 1996 edition of the *Wigan Reporter* had carried a story about a low-flying Chinook helicopter attracting the attention of people in Wigan. It was following (controlling?) a small black triangular-shaped craft a few hundred yards ahead of it.

However, Fowler didn't think that all the triangular UFOs seen over our skies were man-made. There are reports of people seeing huge triangular UFOs, often well-lit, which travel slowly and usually silently. Fowler believed that such craft had an exotic origin.

A CIRCULAR, GLOWING MASS

Jenny Randles, a prolific writer on mysteries of one sort or another, describes an incident that occurred one night in August 1988. A couple were driving at night on a road skirting the northern end of Cannock Chase when they saw a circular mass glowing with a deep reddish colour that pulsed. There was a surrounding cloud or mist, which touched the top of a hedge. A semi-solid object seemed to emerge from the cloud or mist. After about half a minute, the pulsing mass disappeared, only to reappear further north a few seconds later. Then it disappeared. While it was present, the witnesses felt a strange sense of calm and sudden quietness. Signs of damage to the hedge were subsequently found. Randles concludes that the phenomenon was probably an 'atmospheric plasma' or an earth light; and she states that the incident occurred in a geologically faulted area.[3]

MISSING TIME AND 'ALIEN ABDUCTION'

Lee Brickley mentions two missing-time cases from the Cannock Chase area, one from 2002[4] and the other from 2009.[5]

The 2002 case involved Andrew Russell, a plumber from Lichfield. Around 9 p.m. one evening in May, after attending a fitness class in Cannock, he decided to drive home by a more scenic route than his usual one. This should have added only ten minutes to his normal journey time. He had the front windows of his car fully open, and he was listening to BBC Radio 2. While driving through Gentleshaw, a village at the south-eastern end of Cannock Chase, he noticed a constant droning noise. To discover its origin, he stopped his car, and turned off the engine and radio. He couldn't see what was making the noise, and – after five minutes – he resumed his journey. The radio came on again, but all Russell could hear was white noise. He tried to turn down the volume but was unable to do so. He attempted, unsuccessfully, to retune the radio, and then he tried to turn it off, again without success. The noise was getting uncomfortable. He was about to get out of the car when a voice formed out of the white noise and spoke his name, or – perhaps more correctly – *growled* it. The voice roared his name a couple more times and then faded into the white noise. Just after that, he found himself able to operate the radio again. He lit a cigarette and pondered what had just happened. Before he'd finished the cigarette, he heard the droning sound again. He resumed his journey at a slow pace, looking out for aircraft or anything that might explain the droning sound. As he approached Shaw Lane, a road going off to his right, he felt impelled to go that way. Once he was on the lane, he noticed three glowing red lights dancing very rapidly around the sky. Initially, they didn't seem to be in formation. But over the next ten minutes or so he realised that they were moving in some sort of pattern and that they appeared to have noticed him. Then, they came much closer to him, arranged themselves in a triangular pattern, and projected a red, laser-like beam at him, which blinded him for what seemed like a few seconds. Glancing at the clock in his car, he noticed that the time was 2.15 a.m., some four hours later than he would have expected. It seems that the 'loss of time' occurred when he was blinded by the beam, because when he was receiving white noise messages from the car's radio, there were many other cars on the road, and night hadn't completely fallen.

Brickley adds that on the night of Russell's experience, there were also two other reports of red lights being seen in the sky, one from Brownhills and one from Stafford. Those towns are near, but not on, Cannock Chase. It's also worth noting that although Russell's experience occurred while he was driving through a part of Cannock Chase, it seems that he wasn't in a wooded part of it at the time.

The 2009 case involved a young man (precise age unspecified) named Mark, who lived in Heath Hayes. He and two friends, Paul and Ian, were walking home from a birthday party in Pye Green in the early hours of a misty morning. (Brickley doesn't specify the month.) They decided to shorten their route by cutting through a small section of woodland. (Unfortunately, Brickley doesn't specify its precise location.) They were reportedly panicked by a flash of light overhead and a thunderous bang, whereupon they fell to the ground and then felt paralysed, as if they were being pinned down. After less than a minute, Paul and Ian managed to stand up. They discovered that Mark was missing. Despite searching the woods, calling his name, they couldn't find him. Within about an hour, they alerted some friends, who assisted with the search for a while, but to no avail. At 7 a.m., one of those friends, Elaine, rang Paul and Ian to say that she'd found Mark, in a state of shock. Paul and Ian went to Elaine's home. Mark was standing in her front garden, shaking badly and staring blankly at the sky. Elaine explained that he'd been there since she'd arrived home from the search. Paul and Ian carried him into the house, to warm him up, since he was very cold and stiff. After about another ten minutes of shaking, he collapsed on to the carpeted floor. Two hours later, he seemed to return to normal, but his mind seemed to be blank for what had happened after he saw the light and heard the loud bang in the woods.

Mark went on to experience flashbacks, which often left him feeling off-balance and disoriented. He informed Brickley that one of these 'visions' entailed his being strapped down on a black table in a sort of shadowy operating theatre, with an 'evil presence', dressed in black, watching over him and whispering continuously in a language that he couldn't understand. The figure had bright yellow eyes and teeth that were shining white and sharp. Its appearance therefore differed from that of the classic 'Grey' aliens that feature in many abduction accounts. However, as in many other reported abductions, the proceedings entailed an uncomfortable medical-type examination.

In describing Mark's experiences, Brickley seems to be referring to more than just unpleasant, intrusive recollections (flashbacks). If I've understood him correctly, he's saying that Mark felt that he was undergoing repeat performances of the abduction ordeal. However, Brickley notes that, over time, Mark learned to control the visions more effectively.

Author Albert Budden, for one, questions whether such reports reflect actual abductions by aliens.[6] He contends that electric and magnetic fields can induce suitably sensitised people to experience hallucinations with a ghostly or UFO theme. One of the cases he cites is from Australia, and concerns a Maureen Puddy, who had a history of anomalous experiences. In February 1973, she undertook a fairly long car journey to meet UFO investigators Judith Magee and Paul Norman. During the journey, she had a brief vision of a 'spaceman' in her car. Norman and Magee were waiting for her when she arrived. When Magee touched the bodywork of Puddy's car, she (Magee) experienced a strong electric shock, presumably meaning that a static electric charge had discharged itself through her. (Budden quotes from an anonymous source that claims that unexpectedly high magnetic fields were detected in Puddy's car, in the vicinity of the front seats.) The investigators sat with Puddy in her car, to conduct the interview. As she was telling them about seeing the spaceman, she broke off to say that she was seeing him again. However, Magee and Norman couldn't see him. Puddy said that the figure had walked towards the car and was standing in front of it. Norman got out and went to the front of the car, after which Puddy explained that the spaceman had moved back to let him pass. Then, she apparently saw the figure beckoning to her, after which it appeared to melt away into some bushes. Puddy then screamed that she was being abducted, and she gave details of the interior of a flying saucer in which she found herself. Eventually, she returned to her normal state.

Clearly, the Puddy case suggests that at least some abduction experiences are purely subjective events. However, even if they have no objective, physical reality, it's possible that an external intelligence induces people to have such experiences. Furthermore, since some cases involve more than one person, they aren't all easily accounted for in terms of fantasy-proneness.

BIGFOOT SIGHTINGS

Over the years, people in forested areas of the USA and Canada, such as the Pacific Northwest, have reported encounters with tall, stocky ape-like creatures with some human features. They're known, in the singular, as 'bigfoot' or 'sasquatch'. The word 'bigfoot' is often given a capital 'B'. But since it's used as a common noun, and isn't the name given to one particular creature, I prefer to render it with a lower-case 'b'. (The plural form of 'bigfoot' is 'bigfoots', not 'bigfeet'!) Similar creatures have reportedly been encountered elsewhere – for example, in the Himalayas (where they've been called 'yetis'), and in Australia (where they've been dubbed 'yowies'). But there's controversy about the status of bigfoots, yetis and yowies, and their existence isn't officially recognised. It's been suggested, for example, that yeti sightings have been generated by bears walking on their hind legs, and that hoaxing lies behind some of the North American bigfoot reports. Coincidentally or not, bigfoot phenomena have been reported in areas associated with other types of strange occurrence, such as UFO sightings; and judging from some reports, there may be paranormal aspects to bigfoot manifestations themselves. Indeed, if the stranger bigfoot reports can be believed, it seems that some of these entities, at least, aren't normal flesh-and-blood creatures.

Although there are reports of bigfoot encounters occurring during daylight, they're more common at night. The majority of experiences don't entail actual sightings. Rather, people camping or walking in wooded areas might hear loud creature calls that seem to be of neither animal nor human origin, or they might hear loud crashing sounds coming from the bushes. Witnesses might notice an overwhelmingly disgusting smell. (The generation of such an odour by bigfoots could be a way of repelling intruders.) Witnesses might have a strong feeling of being watched, and they might experience a high level of apprehension, inducing them to leave the area. (It's been speculated that bigfoots produce this effect by emitting infrasound.) Large footprints or traces of hair might be found. Large piles of excrement might be seen. In the case of homesteads next to large tracts of forest, there might be a loss of livestock, or fruit might disappear from trees. (Bigfoots are considered to be omnivores.) Food items might go missing from outdoor freezers.

People may find the behaviour of bigfoots intimidating, but reports suggest that they don't usually inflict any physical harm on people. According to Thom Powell, a North American bigfoot researcher, it seems that, on rare occasions, they'll take advantage of lapses in adult supervision to interact with children.[7] But he notes that if a bigfoot takes a child somewhere, it will always return it. He states that, by all appearances, such behaviour is quite benign, or even friendly, and that he's unaware of any indication of violent or sexual intent on the part of the creatures in their interaction with children. He cites reports of bigfoots coming to the aid of humans. For example, he mentions an instance, related to him by a woman called Dora Bradley, who'd had a succession of bigfoot encounters in the vicinity of her childhood home in Montgomery County, Missouri.[8] On the night in question, she was anxiously awaiting the arrival home of her father, who had an alcohol problem. She feared that he might have crashed his pick-up vehicle. Looking through a window, she saw him cradled in the arms of a bigfoot. The creature set him down and then disappeared. Her father was drunk. He'd had an accident and was in pain. His wrecked vehicle was subsequently found 3 miles away.

If flesh-and-blood bigfoots exist, it's conceivable that populations of them have managed to survive, largely undetected, in the large forests that cover parts of North America. But it's much harder to believe that a population of such creatures is resident on England's Cannock Chase, or indeed in any other part of the overpopulated and relatively deforested British Isles. Compared with the forests of, say, the Pacific Northwest, Cannock Chase is a very small area. And, as already noted, it's close to towns and is criss-crossed by roads and tracks. Yet there are reports of people seeing bigfoot-like creatures on, or near, the Chase. Indeed, Nick Redfern claims to have on file some thirty or forty such reports, spanning more than 130 years.[9] Of course, some of these stories could be mischievous inventions, or it may be that pranksters were prancing around in gorilla suits. Another possibility is that the witnesses succumbed to misperception, such as mistaking deer for stranger creatures. Alternatively, these sightings may have been paranormal experiences, involving apparitions or transient materialisations rather than flesh-and-blood animals. At any rate, the following are some examples, including one from a location a few miles north of Cannock Chase.

JACKIE HOUGHTON'S EXPERIENCE

Nick Redfern describes an experience that a motorist, Jackie Houghton, reportedly had around 1 a.m. on 18 February 1995 as she was driving across Cannock Chase on the road linking Cannock and Rugeley (the A460, I presume).[10] However, it's not clear whether Redfern had any direct contact with the witness. At any rate, Houghton was supposedly approaching the turning for Slitting Mill when a large, shambling creature stepped out on the road, about 200 yards ahead of her. She swerved her car and felt that she was lucky not to have hit the entity. It was man-like, tall, very hairy and had self-illuminating red eyes. It immediately vanished into the darkness.

According to Redfern, Houghton made her journey after working a shift at a restaurant in Stafford. It's possible, therefore, that she was rather tired at the time, and that fatigue played a role in her experience.

GAVIN'S TALE

A man, whom Redfern refers to as Gavin, informed him about an experience that allegedly occurred on a winter's night in 1997, which is ambiguous, because it could mean either the beginning or end of 1997, both of which would have been winter.[11] Gavin was reportedly parked in his car with his girlfriend, near the Glacial Boulder, a well-known attraction on Cannock Chase.[12] They were engaging in some intimacy when Gavin's girlfriend let out a scream. A large, hairy man was standing on top of the boulder, waving his arms in a crazed fashion at the sky. Gavin quickly got into the driving seat and roared away, but not before the hairy man had jumped on to the bonnet of the car, where he remained for five minutes before being thrown to the ground! In his rear-view mirror, Gavin noticed that the figure quickly got back on its feet and ran off.

Of course, Gavin may have invented this tale. Even if he didn't, it's perhaps speculative to class this as a sighting of a bigfoot-type creature, since the descriptive details are sparse. If the creature had been a fully-grown flesh-and-blood bigfoot of the type reportedly seen in the Pacific Northwest of the USA and Canada, the bonnet of Gavin's car would have presumably been dented by its great weight. But there's no mention of that in the story relayed by Redfern. And like many of the other accounts cited in this chapter, this is a report from just one witness, and therefore not highly evidential. Assuming that she existed, it would have been interesting to know what Gavin's girlfriend had to say about the story.

Redfern briefly alludes to another driver, Craig Blackmore, who reportedly had a somewhat similar experience to that of Gavin and his girlfriend. While he was driving on Cannock Chase late one night in 2002, a bigfoot-like creature lunged at his vehicle.[13] But could this have been a misinterpreted collision with a deer that was crossing the road?

'BIGFOOT ALMOST MADE ME LOSE MY BABY'

As noted, it's possible that bigfoot reports from Cannock Chase have been generated by pranksters clad in gorilla suits. Dramatically entitled 'Bigfoot almost made me lose my baby', an article in the *Cannock Chase Post* claimed, in March 2006, that, 'Police chiefs [had] hit out at the dangers posed by [a] spoof "Bigfoot" craze after a teenager almost lost her baby when a joker clad in a gorilla suit jumped in front of her car.' According to the article, hoaxers had been tempted by the paper's offer of a free meal for anyone who caught 'the elusive Chase Bigfoot' on film! But there was no mention in the article of anyone being apprehended for perpetrating the supposed hoax, or of anyone admitting to it. Therefore, the notion that the sighting involved someone in a gorilla suit may have been pure conjecture.

ENCOUNTER NEAR CHARTLEY CASTLE

Nick Redfern mentions a story told to him in 2001 by a man whom he refers to as Mick Dodds.[14] One night in 1986, Dodds and his wife were driving near Chartley Castle, about 5 miles north of Cannock Chase, when a huge stag ambled slowly across the road in front of them, causing Dodds to brake hard. Then, a creature looking like a large chimpanzee bounded after the stag, coming on to the road from a field on the couple's right. It stopped suddenly, halfway across the road, looked at the terrified couple and charged their car. But it backed away at the last moment. Putting the car into reverse gear, Dodds inadvertently stalled the engine. As he tried to restart it, he flooded it (the carburettor, I presume). The couple were briefly stranded on the road. For about twenty seconds, the creature stared at them. It made two further charges at the car, and then headed off in the direction that the stag had gone. Dodds wondered whether he and his wife had experienced some form of time displacement.

WOLVES AND WEREWOLVES

An article in the *Birmingham Post* (28 June 2006) stated that, 'Motorists on Junction 10A of the M6, near Cannock, [had] jammed Highways Agency helplines on Wednesday morning, with reports of a "wolf-like creature" racing between lanes at rush hour.' The 3-foot-long creature was described as being grey-ish-black. The witnesses apparently thought they'd seen a wolf, but Highways Agency staff stated that it was likely to have been a husky. Nick Redfern notes that the same week that the wolf story emerged, a report surfaced about the mysterious killing of a former feral cat owned by a couple from Norton Canes (some 3 miles south of Cannock Chase). Its body was found in a field.[15] A vet told the couple that it had experienced a devastating blow on its side, probably from a large dog.

Redfern relates an experience that was supposedly described to him in the summer of 2006 by a man he refers to as Jim Broadhurst.[16] The event had reportedly occurred four days previously. Broadhurst and his wife were walking on Cannock Chase (the precise location isn't specified) when they saw what looked like a large wolf about 150 feet away. It was striding purposefully through dense woodland. The couple were seized with terror when the creature suddenly stopped and looked intently in their direction. Their terror was then greatly amplified when it reared up on its hind legs and backed away into the trees. (It was no doubt its rearing up on its hind legs that exacerbated the couple's terror, not its backing away.)

An article in the *Stafford Post* (26 April 2007) mentioned the West Midlands Ghost Club, which had reportedly been contacted by a number of people who claimed to have seen a hairy wolf-type creature walking on its hind legs around the German Cemetery. But, somewhat contradictorily, the article stated that, 'Several of [the witnesses] claim the creature sprang up on its hind legs and ran into the nearby bushes when it was spotted.'

AN ALLEGED WEREWOLF ENCOUNTER NEAR A GOLF COURSE

Lee Brickley cites a dramatic werewolf story in his book on the Cannock Chase phenomena.[17] In 2012, he was contacted by a Mr Hilton, who described some events that had allegedly occurred several years previously, when Hilton was 37 and working as a French language interpreter with a Birmingham-based company. Along with his wife and daughter, he'd only recently moved to Gentleshaw, which is on the south-eastern fringe of Cannock Chase. He wasn't then familiar with the local folklore.

On the evening of Thursday, 12 February 2004, Hilton, his wife and daughter visited a pub in Hazelslade. Hilton got talking to a couple of men, who invited him to join them for a game of golf the next day. He accepted, and went along to the golf course that day, arriving about 10.10 a.m. Brickley doesn't specify its name, but I think he may be referring to the golf course of Beau Desert Golf Club, which is north of Hazelslade and is surrounded by woodland.

Hilton and his new friends were close to finishing their game when they heard screaming coming from the woods. They ran in the direction of the sounds. Hilton heard his name being called by someone who sounded like his wife. That proved to be the case. His distressed wife fell into his arms and said something about a werewolf, which he initially took to be nonsense. She went on to explain that after he'd left the house earlier that day, their daughter had suggested that they make him a packed lunch and take it to the golf course. They tried to phone him but got no response. When they eventually found the golf course, it was only 11.30 a.m., so Hilton's wife suggested to their daughter that they walk along a path that seemed to go round to the other side of the golf course, where it was likely that they would meet him. As his wife was explaining this, Hilton realised that Emily, their daughter, wasn't present. His wife then explained that when they were on the path, they'd heard rustling noises from the bordering thorn bushes and weeds, and they'd quickened their pace. But whatever was causing the noises kept up. Suddenly, they were stopped dead in their tracks by a 'monster'. It grabbed Emily and ran off into the trees, which was when Hilton's wife started screaming.

Hilton asked which way the entity had gone. His wife pointed, and the four of them ran that way. They shouted Emily's name, and eventually heard her shout back. Hilton then spotted her. She was on the ground, trying to get to her feet. Standing over her, on its hind legs, was a howling, hairy creature. When it detected Hilton's presence, it darted away at what he estimated was well over 30 miles an hour. He described it as looking like a huge dog from the waist down, but like a toned man from the waist up, albeit with a wolf-like head, with salivating ooze dripping from large white fangs! However, it was gone by the time that his wife and two friends arrived on the scene.

Emily was semi-conscious, covered in dirt and had a bleeding gash on her left arm. The Hiltons went to a local hospital, where the wound was cleaned and sealed with glue, obviating the need for stitches. Emily had little recall of the traumatic event: she remembered walking along the path and hearing noises in the bushes, after which everything was fuzzy.

Brickley got to meet Emily when he interviewed Mr Hilton, and he saw her scar. She was nearly 20 then. She revealed to Brickley that, three weeks after the incident, she started noticing thick hairs growing on the back of her left hand. Medical advice was sought, and it was eventually deemed that she was suffering from congenital adrenal hyperplasia (CAH). She was prescribed some steroid tablets. Back home, the hair was shaved off, and never came back.

Some two years after the incident, Mr Hilton obtained copies of Emily's medical records in connection with an unrelated matter. I presume that Brickley was able to see them. He states that they confirm that Emily had been at a hospital on the relevant date, with a wound that was glued, and that CAH was subsequently diagnosed, although her problem cleared up before a follow-up appointment. It's not clear from Brickley's discussion of the case whether he actually spoke to Mrs Hilton.

Brickley notes that, according to mythology, if someone is attacked by a werewolf, and the skin is pierced, the person can become one. He remarks that if Emily's hair growth problem wasn't related to her being wounded by the werewolf, it's an extraordinary coincidence.

If the facts of this case are as described, a possible explanation is that the werewolf was a paranormal manifestation (a transient materialisation), and that it was orchestrated in line with folklore belief about werewolves. As for the abnormal hair growth that Emily subsequently experienced, could it be that it was some sort of temporary reaction to the trauma that she'd endured?

BIG CATS

A BBC internet article, dated 10 February 2003, described Cannock Chase as a 'veritable big cat hotspot [where] there have been many supposed sightings over the last few months.'[18] It stated that witnesses had reported seeing a large black cat with a long tail, and that the village of Stretton, a few miles west of Cannock Chase, was also a regular haunt of the creature, which was the suspected killer of two geese.

An article in the *Birmingham Post* (29 March 2006) referred to a Miss S. Thomas of Hednesford, who claimed that, eleven years previously, she'd come across what she thought was a domestic kitten on the Chase. It looked as if it had been 'dumped', she reported, 'and we took pity on it and took it home.' It grew quickly and was soon larger than a domestic cat. It didn't lie down like a domestic cat, and instead of purring normally, 'it sort of growled'. Eventually, it attacked Miss Thomas's daughter while the latter was asleep, leaving her with a nasty cut. Miss Thomas 'took [the cat] to live outside, but it soon disappeared.' She presumed that it had returned to the Chase.

The same issue of the *Birmingham Post* reported that a man – who didn't want to be named – had photographed the remains of what he believed was a big cat while out walking on the Chase that week. According to the article, the pictures showed a skull that was too large to be that of a domestic animal. The man was quoted as saying that the fangs were 'enormous' and definitely not those of a dog or fox. Nearby, there were reportedly a few other bones, and a trap, secured to a tree, with a bone caught in it.

During a visit to Cannock Chase in April 2008, I spoke to a woman who was walking her dogs. She told me of an occasion, some ten years previously, when she'd seen what she took to be a big cat while she was driving in the area. It crossed a road and jumped over a hedge. And she indicated that about four years after that, she'd had a UFO sighting in the area (from Castle Ring, if I remember rightly), featuring three triangular objects that were in formation.

Big cat sightings are widespread throughout the UK.[19] Therefore, without confirmation from reliable statistics, it might be wrong to assume that Cannock Chase gets more than its fair share. Indeed, the aforementioned BBC internet article states (no doubt with a degree of hyperbole) that '20 miles down the road in a village near Tamworth, sightings are so frequent that everyone's got a tale … to tell'.

From a sceptical point of view, it could be argued that there's no real mystery about supposed big-cat sightings in the UK, and that they're explicable in terms of misperception, misinterpretation, 'mass hysteria' and hoaxing. Hoaxing could take the form of invented sighting reports, or the fabrication of physical traces.

For those believing that big-cat sightings are generated by essentially normal, flesh-and-blood big cats, there are several (not mutually exclusive) possibilities: (1) they may have been living on our islands, largely unobserved, for centuries; (2) they may have been deliberately released from captivity by their owners; or (3) they could be large felines that have somehow escaped from captivity.

Others might favour explanations with a more paranormal flavour. For example, it could be that many out-of-place big cats are 'interdimensional' beings – entities that are able to enter our world from some sort of parallel world or alternative reality. Paranormal theories are discussed at some length in Chapter 10.

THE 'PIG-MAN'

It's no secret that Nazi doctors carried out unethical experiments on prisoners during the time of the Third Reich, and it's well recognised that government agencies in more recent times have sanctioned reprehensible experiments on animals and humans. Lee Brickley describes four alleged sightings of pig-like humans on Cannock Chase and mentions the possibility that they involved hybrids arising from such research.[20] However, if the sightings truly occurred, I think it's most unlikely that they involved flesh-and-blood human-pig hybrids.

INCIDENT AT CASTLE RING

Around 10 p.m. one evening in October 1993, an unnamed middle-aged couple were walking their dog around Castle Ring when they spotted a strange-looking man limping slowly towards them. When he moved from the embankment on to the moon-lit path, they noticed that he had an over-sized, elongated head, huge pointy ears, and a pink snout-like nose protruding from an evil-looking face.

Of course, one might wonder whether this was a prankster wearing a horror mask. At any rate, the couple supposedly fled to their car. As soon as they'd engaged their seatbelts, they heard a squealing noise from behind them, and they sped out of the car park. But it's conceivable, of course, that the squealing noise had been pre-recorded, and was being played by a hoaxer from a 'ghetto blaster' or similar device.

A CYCLIST'S EXPERIENCE

In the spring of 2005, a female cyclist stopped for a breather after a 5-mile ride around the Chase. Brickley doesn't specify the precise location. She heard rustling coming from her left, from just inside the tree line. She saw, kneeling in the dirt, what she described as 'the most loathsome, hideous and unprepossessing monstrosity ever to [have plagued] the woodland of England'. However, from Brickley's brief mention of her encounter, it's not clear whether she explicitly stated that the creature had pig-like features.

Speaking personally and slightly off topic, I have to say that I don't find pigs in any way hideous or disgusting. On the contrary, I think they're attractive creatures; and they have my sympathy, given the appalling treatment that they tend to suffer at the hands of humans.

SIGHTINGS IN 2011

A 17-year-old student, whom Brickley refers to as John, was sitting alone in his Nissan vehicle in a car park (precise location not specified) on Cannock Chase one night in 2011. His was the only car there. After fiddling with his mobile phone for a few minutes, he turned on the car's ignition, and his headlights came on. He saw the 'Pig-Man' staring at him, about 20 metres away. (Unfortunately, Brickley doesn't specify what it was about the figure that merited its being described as such.) Its fiendish gaze terrified John, and he quickly departed. He drove to another car park (location not specified), a good 3 miles away, and switched off his engine. Trembling from his recent fright, he tried to phone some friends, but found that he didn't have a signal. He was about to get out of his car, to see if that would help him get a signal, when – to his horror – he saw the 'Pig-Man' again, just metres away, staring blankly. However, he got away without harm.

As Brickley notes, John's story suggests that there's a paranormal aspect to 'Pig-Man' sightings, since it would have been impossible for any normal creature to cover, on foot, and during the same time, the distance that John had travelled from the first car park to the second one. However, Brickley explains that John and his friends often used car parks on Cannock Chase as meeting places. Therefore, I don't think we can rule out the possibility that John was the victim of a prank involving a couple of friends wearing horror masks.

OTHER STRANGE CREATURES

SNAKES

A strange snake-like creature was reportedly seen on Cannock Chase in the summer of 1976, not far from the village of Slitting Mill. The witness told Nick Redfern about the sighting in 1995.[21] About 6 or 7 feet long, the creature emerged from the surface of a small pool and basked on the bank for at least twenty minutes before sliding back into the water. It appeared to have flippers or small feet near the front. Since the end of the creature didn't come fully out of the water, the witness couldn't tell whether there were also flippers or feet there.

An article in the *Birmingham Post* (20 September 2006) stated that, in March 2006, ramblers had reported seeing a 14-foot snake near Birches Valley on the Chase. An article in the *Cannock Chase Post* (7 May 2009) stated that a rambler had contacted the newspaper the week before to report having spotted a python-sized creature near the German Cemetery. He described it as brightly coloured, with a powerful head. The article noted that pet pythons can grow to a huge length and have been known to be dumped by unthinking owners. In December 2008, an article in the *Cannock Chase Post* reported that two dead pythons had been found hanging from a tree in Chasewater Park (a few miles south of Cannock Chase) the previous week.

A DISTURBED CAMPSITE

Nick Redfern refers to an informant called Tom who had camped in the woods near the German Cemetery with two friends in the summer of 2005. After setting up camp, they went away to buy some provisions. When they returned, they found that items of theirs had been flung about, as if by a large and irate animal. Then, around 2 a.m., they were jolted awake by a hideous scream coming from the woods. The 'following day' (I wonder whether Redfern actually meant later that same day), they went away for more provisions, only to find their tent gone when they returned. However, their other possessions were as they had left them.[22]

LARGE DOGS

As already noted, some of the sightings of strange creatures on Cannock Chase may have been paranormal experiences. In an article in the August 2007 edition of *Fate* magazine, Nick Redfern related that a man was driving over the Chase late one evening in 1972 when he saw a ball of glowing blue light hit the ground ahead of him amid a torrent of bright sparks. He slowed down. Approaching the approximate area where the light had descended, he saw a very large, menacing-looking dog looming before him. After twenty to thirty seconds, it headed for some tall trees, but without taking its eyes off him. Some two or three weeks later, a close friend of the witness was killed, in horrific circumstances, in an industrial accident. Although it could be just coincidental, it ties in with the folklore belief that sightings of ghostly black dogs can be portents of death.[23]

In another article, Redfern described an experience that had reportedly befallen a man who was walking around Castle Ring one morning in December 1991. He noticed a small area of dense fog and went towards it. When he got within about 20 feet of it, he felt his hair become 'static and electrified', and he experienced an intense smell of burning metal. A monstrous black dog – about the size of a young horse – loomed out of the fog. The man and the dog slowly backed away from each other, with the latter retreating into the fog. When the man was maybe 150 feet from the fog, he saw a small ball of light zoom in over it and cast down a column of vivid blue light towards it. In an instant, normality was restored – the fog, the ball of light and the dog were all gone.[24]

TROLL-LIKE ENTITIES

Nick Redfern relates a strange experience that reportedly occurred in the early hours of the morning in 1975, although it's not entirely clear whether the testimony he cites was obtained first-hand from Barry and Elaine, the married couple that he mentions.[25] They were in their late twenties at the time and had been at a Christmas party in Penkridge with their two small children. On the way back to their then home in Slitting Mill, their car broke down, close to the village. Barry carried out some checks but couldn't discern what was wrong. He proposed leaving Elaine and the children in the car while he ran home to get her vehicle, in which he would return to collect them. However, he didn't get to execute that plan, because Elaine let out a scream, having seen a small figure running across the road in front of them at high speed. It was followed by a second one and then a third. In the moonlight, they looked to her like small naked, hairy, hunchbacked men with large hooked noses. As Barry recalled, the creatures slowly approached them. But it seems that for a period after that, he and his wife were left with no clear recollection of what had happened. The next thing he recalled was that it was about 2 a.m. and that the car started with no problem. It seems that the children had no memory of these strange happenings.

HUMAN APPARITIONS

Over the years, I've come across various reports of people seeing human apparitions on or around Cannock Chase. Since we don't have comparative statistical data, it's hard to know whether the area plays host to a disproportionately high number of cases. But the following are some examples.

A PHANTOM MAN, HORSE AND CARRIAGE

At lunchtime on 29 July 2005, Cherill Penton, whose surname is now Royce-Dexter, had an experience that included not only a phantom man but also an apparitional horse and carriage. That day, she posted a report of it to the internet forum of the Paranormal Awakening Scientific Study Association, a group that she'd co-founded. At the time of the event, she was in her car, at the junction of Borough Lane and Horsey Lane in Rugeley, a little to the east of Cannock Chase. She was waiting to turn left. She heard the sound of a horse's hooves clopping on the road to her right. The sounds appeared louder than usual. After what seemed like a long wait, a horse and carriage, with a single driver, appeared in front of her, out of nowhere. The driver looked at her, tipped his hat and smiled. Then, the vision vanished suddenly.

A SHAPE-SHIFTING, VANISHING PASSENGER

Lee Brickley recounts two incidents that were related to him by a Mr Bird (pseudonym) very soon after they happened, some ten to thirteen years ago.[26] The first one allegedly occurred when Bird was driving, early one morning, on Stile Cop Road near Rugeley. He saw a woman at the roadside, staring blankly into the road ahead.

He turned his car round at the next junction, drove back to her, and asked whether she needed any assistance. She nodded, and he offered her a lift. Without saying anything, she got into the back of his car and clicked the seatbelt into place. She seemed to be about 25. Bird chatted away, but she said nothing. Then, to his horror, he noticed, in his rear-view mirror, that she'd turned into an old, ugly and evil-looking witch-like figure, dressed in rags. He brought his car to a halt and turned around, only to discover that she'd vanished.

Subsequently, according to what Bird told Brickley, he saw the woman again on Stile Cop Road, although someone else had stopped to pick her up. But Bird reportedly followed close behind this other vehicle, expecting to see the woman in the back seat vanish. Instead, though, the vehicle itself, along with its driver and passenger, 'faded to dust' (Brickley's words).

Brickley discovered that, in 1984, Cannock Chase Council had opened a cemetery beside Stile Cop Road, because many local burial grounds were at capacity. Its entrance is very close to where Bird claimed to have had his sightings.

GHOSTLY ROMAN SOLDIERS

Towards the end of 2012, Lee Brickley was contacted by a 71-year-old woman from Norton Canes, who reported having seen what she took to be an apparition of a Roman soldier in the Birches Valley area of Cannock Chase. Unfortunately, no date is given for the sighting, which occurred on a Monday afternoon, around 4 p.m. She was out with her dog, which acted strangely, by sitting at her feet, unwilling to move. It started barking at what, to her, was an empty field. Then she saw what appeared to be a man, dressed in red and silver uniform, walking towards her. But after about twenty seconds, the figure vanished before her eyes.

Within a matter of weeks of getting this report, Brickley received another, from Stanley Gregg, a 42-year-old mechanic. Around 4 a.m. on 12 October 2012, he took his dog for a walk in the Birches Valley area. He spotted a strange figure moving between the trees. As he approached it, he noticed that it was clad in old military uniform, like that in the film *Gladiator*. Before he was close enough to see the figure's face, it was gone.[27]

A STRANGE VISION AT CASTLE RING

Nick Redfern describes a strange dream-like or hallucinatory experience that was related to him by a woman whom he refers to as Pauline Charlesworth.[28] On a bright day in July 1986, she went by herself to Castle Ring for a picnic. She laid out a blanket on the ground and, for over an hour, sat reading. Then, all the ambient noises, such as the whistling of birds, completely stopped. She saw a man running directly towards her. He was fairly short, was clad in animal skins and had a matted beard, filthy long hair and a 'dumpy' face. In his right hand, there were deer antlers that had been fashioned into a dagger-like weapon. He looked at her curiously, in what she deemed to be a disturbing and sinister way, and he seemed to speak to her in a language that she didn't understand. It was as if he were angry and firing questions at her. She heard other voices approaching, and then, through a break in the trees, came some thirty or forty similarly clad people, mainly men. They were chanting. They sat down around the edge of the Ring.

A man who was much taller than the others, and whom Pauline took to be the leader of the group, marched over to her and said something unintelligible. He waved his arm curtly, which she took to be an order to get out of the circle. She retreated to the tree line and looked on, transfixed with terror, for more than fifteen minutes as the strange people continued to chant and sway. Then, out of the sky, a bizarre creature slowly dropped to the ground. It prowled around the Ring for a minute, staring at the assembled people, emitting hideous loud shrieks. As Pauline recalled, it was about 4 feet tall, human in shape, but with oily, greasy, black skin, thin limbs, red glowing eyes and large leathery wings. Suddenly, it was pounced on and wrestled to the ground by seven or eight of the men, who bound it with ropes. In its struggle, it tore into their flesh with its claws, but they finally subdued it and then dragged it into the forest, with the rest of the party following. At that point, the strange atmosphere started to lift and eventually things returned to normal. For several minutes, Pauline was too afraid to move, but then she gathered her things and ran to her car.

The book that Pauline was reading at Castle Ring was a fantasy novel called *Mythago Wood* by Robert Holdstock. Redfern concedes that a sceptic might interpret Pauline's experience as a bizarre dream or nightmare brought on by reading it. But she reportedly believed that she'd experienced a unique glimpse into the distant past of the area.

OCCULT RITUALS

Given that Cannock Chase is a rural oasis adjacent to an urban sprawl, it wouldn't be surprising if it attracted occultists who wished to practise rituals, of either 'white' (benign) or 'black' (evil) intent, away from public gaze. Obviously, though, it's hard to know whether such activities have any bearing on the aforementioned anomalous phenomena (UFO sightings, apparitions, etc.).

At any rate, Nick Redfern cites testimony suggesting that occult rituals have been carried out in the area.[29] In 1999, an informant, referred to as Frank, told him that the previous year, while walking his Labrador dog near the village of Brocton, he'd come upon the remains of five fully grown foxes, which were laid out in a circle on a patch of grassy ground. About 6 or 7 feet from the bodies, there were the remains of a large candle. In the late 1970s, a couple (whom Redfern interviewed in 1999) came across a dead deer on the Chase, somewhere between the German Cemetery and the British Telecom tower at Pye Green. Its major organs had been removed and were laid out on the ground in a clearly delineated pattern; and it appeared that the carcass and organs had remained completely untouched by the other animals inhabiting the area. A member of the Staffordshire Constabulary informed Redfern that he'd investigated the mutilation and killing of several ducks and other water birds at Shugborough Hall, near Milford, on the northern fringe of the Chase. And Redfern states that, in the mid-1960s and in 1981, tales circulated among the staff at Shugborough Hall about wild, hairy men being seen in the nearby woods after the sun had gone down and the moon was full.

COMMENTS

In discussing an area that's deemed to be a hot spot for strange phenomena, it's tempting to include incidents that have occurred not only within it but also relatively close. In the foregoing paragraphs, I've done that myself. For example, I've mentioned Cherill Penton's sighting of an apparitional man and horse-drawn carriage in 2005, which occurred close to, but not actually on, Cannock Chase. And in Chapter 9, I discuss sightings near Woodseaves, Staffordshire, of an entity that's been dubbed the 'Man-Monkey'. The area in question is about 13 miles from Cannock Chase. However, if a significant number of incidents occur beyond the boundaries of a supposed hot spot, one has to ask whether the area itself is in any way unique.

Although the Chase has supposedly been a UFO hot spot for many years, I'm not sure whether the incidence of sightings has actually been any higher than elsewhere. Even if it has, there may be prosaic explanations. Given the publicity that the area has received, people there may have been more inclined to look at the sky and notice aerial objects, whatever their nature. Since it's a fairly rural area, with less light pollution than built-up areas, it might be easier for observers there to notice – and sometimes misinterpret – planets, satellites, aircraft and so on in the night sky.

Many of the stories mentioned above are single-witness accounts, and some of the reports are vague or effectively anonymous (or both), amounting to little more than rumour. The number of stories might seem impressive, but it's conceivable that hoaxers have fabricated tales in line with the local folklore, giving the impression that the locality is seething with 'high strangeness'. But to the extent that the reports are genuine and reflect truly paranormal events, it could be that whatever's behind the phenomena is tricksterish, and that it deliberately crafts them in such a way as to leave uncertainty and doubt about their occurrence and true nature. One way of doing that could be to target single witnesses (precluding corroboration), and leaving few, if any, physical traces.

ENCOUNTER IN DECHMONT WOOD

Livingston, one of the new towns built in Scotland after the Second World War, takes its name from a village that's been incorporated in the new development. The town is situated south of the M8 motorway, which connects Edinburgh with Glasgow.[1] Edinburgh city centre is about 12 miles east-north-east of Livingston, and Glasgow city centre is some 25 miles to the west. The Ordnance Survey's Explorer 349 map (*Falkirk, Cumbernauld & Livingston*) depicts the area at a scale of 1:25,000 (2½in to 1 mile).

Livingston Development Corporation (LDC) was established in 1962 to build, manage and promote the new town. In March 1997, West Lothian Council assumed administrative responsibility of the town, which is the largest in West Lothian.

Between the M8 motorway to the north and the built-up part of Livingston further south, there are two small, grassy hills and a small area of woodland, which is partly coniferous. The hills are Dechmont Law (217m/712ft) and Deer Hill (193m/633ft).

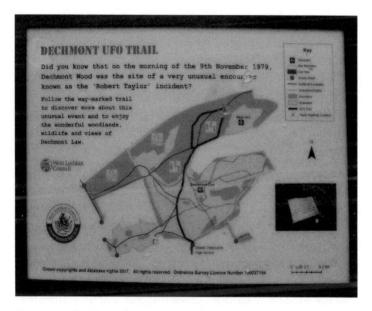

Notice regarding the Dechmont UFO Trail.

The area can be accessed from a free car park beside Deans Community High School. Helpfully, there's a notice there, with a map showing a 'UFO Trail', which leads to the scene of the event that's described below.

Although the woods are visually appealing, they're subject to the drone of traffic from the motorway immediately to their north. Edinburgh Airport is only about 7 miles away, so aircraft contribute to the sound pollution.

On the morning of 9 November 1979, 61-year-old Robert David Taylor, a forestry foreman employed by LDC, reportedly had a traumatic encounter with what he later described as a 'spaceship'. This was in a clearing in the woods to the west of Deer Hill. He was accompanied by his 7-year-old red setter,

Lara. Obviously, we'll never know what she experienced. Indeed, we'll never know exactly what happened to Taylor himself that day, which was a Friday. As in other cases of this type, sources differ about the precise details, and it may be that Taylor himself changed his testimony to some degree over time (perhaps wholly unwittingly). But it's worth emphasising that people acquainted with Bob Taylor, as he was known informally, regarded him as a straightforward type of person, not someone likely to deliberately fabricate a UFO story. He died in March 2007, aged 88.

The press were soon on to the case. I presume that they learned of it from the police, who were involved more or less from the outset, given that Robert Taylor appeared to have been assaulted, albeit in an unusual way. The case received wide coverage.

The area has undergone significant changes over the years. Malcolm Robinson refers to a visit that he made in June 1988.[2] He'd last been there six years previously, but now he noticed that many new houses had been built nearby, that many trees had been felled, that new pathways had been created in the woods, that picnic tables and benches had been installed there and that an adjacent golf course had been extended and now came quite close to the site of Taylor's encounter.

The view from the clearing was more open in 1979, the trees then being shorter than now. Maybe they were planted, several decades ago, to provide a degree of amenity in what's essentially an urban environment.

SOURCES

I never met Bob Taylor, but I visited the site with author and researcher Ron Halliday in August 2018. My principal sources have been the following books:

All three authors have been active investigators in Scotland (although Robinson is now based in southern England), and all were in touch with Bob Taylor. But their depictions of what happened differ in some respects. It seems that Robinson met Taylor several times. Halliday met him in January 1998. By then, Taylor had moved north to Blairgowrie, a town in the former county of Perthshire. He'd had a slight stroke, had suffered a heart attack and had lost his wife, but he confirmed to Halliday that what he'd reported about the 1979 incident was true. It seems that Steuart Campbell also met Taylor face-to-face, but I don't know how many times.

TAYLOR'S BACKGROUND

Campbell's book (p. 145, 149) gives the following details about Bob Taylor: At the time of the incident, he'd been working in LDC's Forestry Department for sixteen years. He contracted viral meningitis in 1965 but made a good recovery. He was admitted to hospital in 1977 with mild hepatitis. At some point, he underwent surgery for repair of a hernia. On another occasion, he had neck surgery in relation to cervical spondylosis. He suffered from angina and high blood pressure and was on medication for the latter. He wasn't normally prone to headaches, dizziness or blackouts, and he had good hearing.

He used glasses for reading. He was a cigarette smoker, but he drank very little alcohol. However, Campbell notes that Taylor had a poor appetite, which he (Taylor) ascribed to the state of his liver. Campbell refers to possible cirrhosis due to previous heavy drinking, but it's not clear whether his mention of past 'heavy drinking' is an inference or something that Taylor admitted to Campbell. At any rate, it seems that Taylor wasn't a heavy drinker around the time of his 1979 experience.

THE ENCOUNTER

As Taylor and his dog approached a clearing in the woods on the morning in question, he was shocked to see a large, hemispherical object there. Robinson (Vol. 1, p. 128) gives the time as around 10.10 a.m. According to Campbell (p. 145), it was around 10.15 a.m. According to Halliday (p. 2), it was around 10.30 a.m. Campbell states that the object seemed to be about 6m in diameter and 4m in height. Its dome was uppermost, and at the bottom there was a flange or rim, resembling the brim of a hat.[3] Some regularly spaced stems protruded vertically from the upper edge of the flange, and were surmounted by propeller-like appendages, although they weren't moving. On the dome, just above the flange, there were regularly spaced circular patches, of a darker colour.

Halliday (p. 2) explains that although some reports say that the object was supported by three thin metal legs, Taylor himself didn't confirm that. Rather, the craft seemed to be 'hovering above the ground' (p. 8).[4] I'll refer to it as an unidentified flying object (UFO).

It was of a dark metallic grey appearance, with numerous bright highlights. Its surface resembled emery paper. As Taylor stared at its 'hull', parts of it seemed to dematerialise, enabling him to see young trees in the background. Seconds later, these transparent patches became opaque again. The only sound that Taylor recalled hearing at that point was Lara's barking.

After a few seconds, two small, spherical objects (0.5–1.0m in diameter) came into view. They had protruding spikes and resembled wartime naval mines. Campbell (p. 145) states that Taylor didn't see where they'd come from. According to Halliday (p. 3), they dropped to the ground, and it appeared to Taylor that they'd come from inside the UFO (which could mean that Taylor *inferred* that they'd come from the UFO but didn't actually see them drop from it). Robinson (Vol. 1, p. 129) gives the impression that Taylor saw them drop from the larger object. At any rate, it seems that their colour and texture matched that of the larger object. Making a distinct plopping sound, they rolled towards Taylor, one to his left, and one to his right. They reached the sides of his boots at the same time and attached themselves to the outside edges of his trousers, just below the pockets. He felt himself being dragged towards the larger object, and he noticed a choking, acrid smell resembling that of burning brake linings. Over the noise of Lara's barking, he heard a sound resembling that of a cane being swished through the air. He then seemed to lose consciousness. His next recollection was of coming to, with his face pressed against the ground. It appears that he'd been unconscious for some twenty minutes. His legs were aching, and he was temporarily unable to walk. Lara was racing about, barking. When Taylor tried to speak to her, he discovered that he'd lost his voice. His throat was very dry, and he was experiencing a burning sensation on his chin. He had a bad headache and felt very sick. The UFO and associated spheres had vanished.

Unable to stand, Taylor crawled on his hands and knees for about 90 metres, back along the way he'd come. Then, he managed to get up and walk, unsteadily, back to his pick-up truck. Because he'd lost his voice, he couldn't speak to his headquarters via the vehicle's two-way radio. According to Halliday (p. 3), he was unable to start the truck. However, Robinson (Vol. 1, p. 129) states that the vehicle had become stuck in a ditch and that Taylor was unable to move it. But that's ambiguous, because it could mean that the vehicle became stuck either prior to, or after, the UFO encounter. But Campbell explains (p. 146) that it was when Taylor tried to leave that his truck became mired in soft ground.

Taylor's home was relatively nearby, in the Deans area of Livingston, and he managed to walk home, during which time he recovered his voice. But according to Campbell (p. 146), he was still aware of the acrid smell,[5] was still feeling sick, and he still felt pain in his chin; and his frontal headache persisted for several hours, and he felt thirsty for two days.

AFTERMATH

Taylor told his wife, Mary, that he'd seen a 'spaceship' in the woods. She was shocked by his appearance and thought that he might be confused. According to Halliday and Robinson, she phoned their GP, Dr Gordon Adams, and her husband's boss, Malcolm Drummond, the head of LDC's forestry department.

Robinson (Vol. 1, p. 130) states that Adams and Drummond soon arrived, whereupon Taylor related what had happened in the woods. Dr Adams examined Taylor. Although he found nothing significantly wrong, he wanted him to have a fuller check-up at a hospital. Robinson states that Taylor and his wife went along to Bangour Hospital[6] with Adams, where Taylor waited for the check-up.

However, Campbell (p. 146) describes the events differently. He states that it was Malcolm Drummond who called a doctor. Drummond arrived at the Taylors' home and spoke to Bob Taylor while the latter was having a bath! Taylor reportedly said that there must have been ground marks where he'd seen the UFO. Drummond set off to look but couldn't find the clearing. Meanwhile, Dr Adams arrived. He examined Taylor and ordered an ambulance to take him to a hospital for a head X-ray and an interview with a psychiatrist.[7] But before he and his wife were collected by the ambulance, Taylor found time to visit the scene of the incident with Drummond, whereupon ground marks were found (discussed below) and the police were called. When Taylor and his wife later got to the hospital, they were kept waiting and eventually left before he could be examined. Campbell notes that Taylor was feeling well, and that the couple wanted to get away for the weekend to visit relatives.[8]

POLICE INVESTIGATION

Campbell (p. 147) explains that in cases of alleged assault, police in Scotland are required to have the relevant clothing forensically examined. It was determined that Taylor's trousers and long johns had been torn in the hip area on each side. One of the tears corresponded to where he had a graze. The tears suggested that the trouser material had been pulled up while Taylor was wearing the trousers. If so, this presumably means that he fell to the ground and was pulled head first towards the UFO.

There was no evidence of helicopter activity in the area on the day of the incident or the day before. And there was no sign of a mobile crane that might have lowered something into the clearing.

GROUND MARKS

On p. 148 of his book, Campbell reproduces a police plan of ground marks found at the site of the encounter. There were two parallel tracks, each about 8 feet long, and each with a ladder-like pattern. However, the indentations affected only the grass – the ground below didn't appear to be compressed. In addition, there were forty holes, about 4 inches wide, at an angle of about thirty degrees to the horizontal. They exposed fresh soil.

During his first visit to the site, Campbell saw stacks of PVC pipes in an adjacent field. He discovered that, in the late summer, the local water authority had been laying a cable duct within 100m of the clearing, and he surmised that the workers had stored two stacks of pipes in the clearing. If so, the 'rungs' of the ladder-like impressions may have been produced by the wooden bands that held the stacks together. He suggests that the holes may have been caused by an implement used to remove the bottom timbers of the bands. He traced the men involved in the work, who said that they'd travelled through the clearing, although they denied having stored items there. But Campbell suggests that they were lying, perhaps because they weren't supposed to have used the clearing for storing items. For his part, though, Taylor didn't recall seeing anything lying there during previous visits. In any case, Halliday notes (p. 8) that the ground marks don't seem to relate directly to the UFO that Taylor saw, which seemed to be hovering above the ground, not resting on it.

OTHER SIGHTINGS AROUND THE SAME TIME

Malcolm Robinson (Vol. 1, p. 138) refers to a report in the 20 November 1979 edition of the *Daily Record*, a Scottish tabloid newspaper, concerning the parents of a famous golfer, Bernard Gallagher. Three days after Taylor's experience, they'd reportedly seen a circular UFO with blinking red and white lights above them, close to their West Lothian home. But Robinson doesn't specify the actual location of their home, or how far it was from the site of Taylor's experience. He indicates that the same article also referred to a Mrs Violet Conner. On the day of Taylor's sighting, the 35-year-old had allegedly seen a craft resembling what he'd seen. However, Robinson doesn't indicate where she was when she spotted it.

Ron Halliday (pp. 12–15) cites several witnesses who'd reportedly had UFO experiences around the same time, in the general vicinity of Bob Taylor's encounter. However, I don't know whether all of these reports were obtained first hand by Halliday. His book explains that some names have been changed, to 'preserve the anonymity of witnesses'. But he doesn't specify where he's made such changes. Therefore, I don't know whether the names given below are genuine. To highlight this uncertainty, I've placed each one in quotation marks the first time I've used it.

It's hard to say whether these sightings were directly related to what Taylor experienced. Given that they occurred only a few days after Guy Fawkes Night (5 November), some of them may have been generated by fireworks. Furthermore, Halliday notes that some of the incidents were reported years after the event.

A STRIP OF BRILLIANT LIGHT

At 8 p.m. on the day before Taylor's sighting, a 'Mr A. Ferguson' of Edinburgh was parking his lorry in a lay-by when he allegedly noticed a strip of brilliant light heading towards Dechmont Law. Halliday doesn't specify where Ferguson was at the time, and how close he was to the hill. The report reached Halliday in October 1992, many years after Taylor's experience.

A SILVERY OBJECT WITH FLASHING LIGHTS

Another report that reached Halliday in 1992 was from a 'Mrs E. Scott'. While standing at a bus stop (at an unspecified location), looking towards the Pentland Hills, which are to the south of Edinburgh, she reportedly saw a silvery object with flashing lights. She drew it to the attention of another woman at the bus stop, who also thought that it was unusual. Suddenly, it shot off, at high speed, towards Dechmont Law and disappeared. The witness was unsure of the date but thought that it was either the day of Taylor's experience (9 November 1979) or the day before. It was daylight at the time, but Mrs Scott couldn't recall the exact time of her experience.

Given that we're not told where Mrs Scott was at the time of her sighting, and how far she was from Dechmont Law, her reported claim that the UFO shot off in the direction of the hill should be treated with caution.

A ROTATING CIRCLE OF LIGHTS

At 5.50 p.m. on 8 November 1979, in the Livingston area, 'Mrs Josephine Quigley' and four friends noticed a circle of lights that appeared to be low in the sky and rotating slowly. After two minutes, Mrs Quigley moved away and lost sight of it.

A HOVERING UFO

Two hours after Mrs Quigley's sighting, brothers 'Steven and Alan Little' saw a dome-shaped aerial object near their home at Bellsquarry, Livingston. It was some 400m away from them, over a road, and at an estimated height of 150m above the ground. It had an array of glowing white lights, and pulsating blue and red lights on each side. After several minutes, the whitish glow, which outlined the object, faded. The pulsating lights went out shortly after. The brothers heard no sound from the object.

A TORCH-SHAPED OBJECT

At 8.05 a.m. on 9 November 1979, as 'Graham Kennedy' was driving west on the A89 road, passing Bangour Hospital, he noticed a bright light above and to the left of his car. It came towards him, on a collision course. He swerved to avoid a crash with the orange-coloured object, which was torch-shaped. In doing so, he nearly rammed a car heading the opposite way. Thankfully, both vehicles managed to stop in time. The other driver said that he hadn't seen the object spotted by Kennedy.

A FLASHING, STATIONARY LIGHT

That same morning, and about the same time, a van driver heading west on the A89 towards Broxburn saw a stationary aerial light that seemed too big to be a star or a planet. It flashed on and off intermittently, gradually getting dimmer. Halliday doesn't name the witness.

ANOTHER SIGHTING NEAR BANGOUR HOSPITAL

Around the same time as the van driver's experience, 'Anne MacGregor', a young nurse, alighted from a bus and started to walk along the A89 towards Bangour Hospital. After hearing a hissing noise, she glanced up and saw a bright yellow light. It seemed to be descending over the Deans area of Livingston, which is near Dechmont Law.

A YELLOWISH LIGHT HOVERING OVER THE M8 MOTORWAY

A few minutes after Anne MacGregor's sighting, an unnamed cyclist spotted a bright, yellowish light that seemed to be hovering over the M8 motorway, close to Deer Hill.

SUGGESTED EXPLANATIONS

Speculations about what happened to Bob Taylor have ranged from the sceptical (e.g. that his report was a deliberate fabrication) to the notion that he encountered an exotic craft from 'another dimension'. Strictly speaking, a theory is a formal, systematically elaborated, and internally consistent set of propositions advanced to explain something, whereas a hypothesis (by definition, something less than a thesis) is just one explanatory proposal. In terms of this distinction, the explanatory notions discussed below are for the most part tentative hypotheses, not detailed, well-substantiated theories.

A PUBLICITY STUNT

In a short, sceptical article about the case, Nigel Watson seems to suggest that the incident was fabricated 'to promote [the Livingston] development zone to the nation in a very cheap and rapid manner.'[9] He notes that many people made a 'pilgrimage' to the site, and that it was logical for the local tourist board to capitalise on this. Ron Halliday (pp. 6–7) dismisses this as a fanciful notion. He notes that LDC wouldn't have involved itself in such a stunt, and it would have been unnecessary, since the area was already becoming home to computer and associated industries. He explains that unlike nearby Edinburgh, the area isn't a natural tourist magnet. It's also worth noting that a hoax perpetrated by LDC would almost certainly have been illegal, not least because it would have entailed wasting police time. Furthermore, it's by no means certain that fabricating a UFO or paranormal incident would have attracted the sort of attention that a local authority would welcome. Later in this book, I'll discuss the case of Dering Wood in Kent, where damage has been done by irresponsible visitors who may have been attracted by the wood's reputation for being haunted.

AN EPILEPTIC FIT

Steuart Campbell (pp. 151–52) refers to a Dr Patricia Hannaford, a physician with an interest in the UFO topic. After hearing Bob Taylor's story and interviewing him, she suggested that he'd experienced an isolated epileptic fit. The meningitis he'd suffered years before may have rendered him susceptible to temporal lobe epilepsy. Campbell (p. 152) notes that the strong, unpleasant odour that Taylor experienced, which no one else could smell, and other features (e.g. his period of unconsciousness, his headache and his dry throat) were consistent with an epileptic attack. From that point of view, the UFO and associated mine-like objects that Taylor 'saw' could be interpreted as hallucinations.

However, while accepting that Taylor may have had a fit, Campbell suggests that the visual component of his experience was based on, and triggered by, the planet Venus, and perhaps Mercury as well. At the time of Taylor's experience, these planets were apparently 'rising' to the south-east. A temperature inversion (warm air overlying colder air below) may have led to the refraction (bending) of light, Campbell argues. On this basis, he suggests that the main object (the UFO) was an enlarged image of Venus!

If I haven't expressed Campbell's hypothesis very lucidly, it's because I'm not entirely clear about what he's suggesting. And I have to say that I'm sceptical about it. The object that Taylor described was structured. It wasn't an amorphous blur. Indeed, I think it's easier to construe his sighting as a hallucination than as a mirage, although I'm by no means sure that that's what it was. In any case, there are problems in suggesting that Taylor had an epileptic fit. He didn't have a history of epileptic seizures, and – as Campbell himself notes (p. 152) – when he subsequently underwent examination at a major hospital in Edinburgh, no abnormal brain activity was detected.

BELLADONNA POISONING

In Volume 2 of his *UFO Case Files of Scotland* (pp. 256–64), Malcolm Robinson returns to the Bob Taylor case and discusses another possible medical explanation of Taylor's experience – one suggested to him, in 2010, by a correspondent called David Slater. The latter's hypothesis involves the plant *Atropa belladonna* (commonly known 'belladonna' or 'deadly nightshade'). It's foliage and berries can be extremely toxic when ingested, causing delirium, hallucinations and death. The toxic agents include atropine, scopolamine and hyoscyamine.

According to Robinson, Slater proposed (in an article that he sent to Robinson) that on the morning of 9 November 1979, Taylor either ingested some belladonna berries or possibly rubbed them on his hands, whereupon the juices passed into his system through his skin. The toxins, Slater suggested, induced a hallucinatory UFO experience. As for why Taylor 'saw' what he did, Slater noted that the BBC had aired a new series of *Doctor Who*, titled 'City of Death', beginning on 29 September 1979. The opening sequence featured an alien spacecraft, similar to what Taylor had reported seeing. It was featured again in the final episode, on 20 October, in which a character called out, 'My God, that's a spaceship!' The suggestion, of course, is that a memory, in Bob Taylor's mind, of seeing the fictional spaceship served as the kernel for a belladonna-induced hallucination. But it's questionable whether Taylor watched either of the *Doctor Who* episodes. Robinson contacted a couple of his relatives, who said that he didn't watch *Doctor Who*. However, around the time that the episodes went out, ITV, the rival channel, was off the air because of industrial action. So even though he may not have normally watched the programme, it's conceivable that Taylor did see one, or both, of the relevant *Doctor Who* episodes. But on the basis of his enquiries, Robinson didn't come up with any confirmation that belladonna was present in Dechmont Wood. Furthermore, I think it's unlikely that an experienced forestry worker such as Taylor would have ingested belladonna berries or otherwise rendered himself liable to toxins from the plant.

A MINI-STROKE

Another speculative medical explanation has been proposed by Phill Fenton, who suggests that Taylor's experience occurred at a nearby water treatment plant and *not* in Dechmont Wood. Fenton proposes that Taylor suffered a mini-stroke (a transient ischaemic attack) that left him confused, and that he was exposed to chlorine gas given off by concentrated sodium hypochlorite at the water treatment plant. Fenton suggests that the 'UFO' that Taylor saw was actually a dome-shaped water tank at the site.[10, 11]

A MILITARY DEVICE

Robinson (Vol. 1, pp. 159–61) refers to an email correspondent who mentioned a photograph that he'd seen of a remotely controlled American helicopter-type machine. It was designed to place mines close to enemy tanks and then leave the scene. However, because it was prone to crashing on highways, it was withdrawn. Its appearance was supposedly very similar to that of the craft that Taylor had described. According to the correspondent, whom Robinson doesn't name, shortly after Taylor's encounter, British Aerospace announced that it would cease research and development into such unmanned vehicles.

I must say that I'm very doubtful whether British Aerospace or any branch of the British military would have been testing a prototype device of that kind in an area open to the public and within a stone's throw of the busy M8 motorway. Moreover, the theory doesn't account for aspects of Taylor's experience (e.g. his period of unconsciousness).

AN EXOTIC CRAFT

The aforementioned theories are quite varied, but they're alike in that they're speculative attempts to account for Taylor's experience in prosaic, naturalistic terms. However, Robinson (Vol. 1, p. 137) believes that Taylor saw what he thought he saw, a spaceship, although he suggests that UFOs may come from 'other dimensions' rather than outer space (*ibid.*, pp. 139–40).

There are other possibilities. If time travel is a reality, it's conceivable that Taylor encountered something from the future. Alternatively, his experience could be interpreted as a sort of theatrical display somehow orchestrated by the collective unconscious mind (if such a thing exists) or by a resourceful higher intelligence. From that point of view, the UFO and mine-like objects may have been creations of the moment – transient materialisations – rather than objects with an enduring existence.

COMMEMORATION OF TAYLOR'S EXPERIENCE

Philip Mantle is a West Yorkshire-based UFO researcher and author. Robinson (Vol. 1, p. 143) explains that after a visit, in June 1988, to the scene of Bob Taylor's encounter, he suggested to Robinson that it would be good if the spot could be marked by something to commemorate the incident. That gave impetus to what Robinson and Ron Halliday had already been thinking. Approaches were made to LDC, and a boulder was placed in the clearing in October 1991, with a plaque alluding to the incident. Disappointingly, the plaque didn't actually mention Taylor by name, and within less than a year, one or more vandals had removed it from the boulder. It has since been replaced, although the wording is the same – it still doesn't mention Taylor by name. But there's a plinth beside the boulder, topped with a board giving information about Taylor's encounter and which names him.

COMMENTS

So far as I know, Dechmont Wood hasn't been the setting for any other encounters resembling what Bob Taylor reportedly experienced. Apart from his dog, he was the sole witness. And, as noted above, there are conflicting accounts about what happened afterwards. Furthermore, at least one commentator – Phill Fenton (see above) – questions whether the incident actually occurred in the woods. All told, in evidential terms, this isn't a very strong

Ron Halliday at the site of Robert Taylor's encounter.

case. Admittedly, there seem to have been other UFO sightings in the general area around the time, although it's unclear whether they were related to what Taylor saw. It's possible that if more information had been available, some of them, at least, could have been explained in normal terms (e.g. as misperceived conventional aircraft). Therefore, taking everything into account, I'm undecided about this case: while I find the story intriguing, I don't have a clear idea of what happened to Bob Taylor on the day in question, and I doubt whether we'll ever know for sure what really transpired.

8

RENDLESHAM FOREST

In late December 1980, Rendlesham Forest, Suffolk, became the setting for one of Britain's best-known UFO cases, often referred to as the 'Rendlesham Forest Incident' (RFI). The expression is a misnomer, because there were *multiple* incidents, spanning several days. But since the term and the associated abbreviation have become so popular, I'll use them myself, in good part to differentiate between the events of late December 1980 (the RFI proper) and events preceding and following it. Arguably, researchers will risk missing the bigger picture if they focus exclusively on the RFI itself.

It wasn't until 1983 that the RFI received wide publicity. There are conflicting versions of what happened, and the case remains a focus of controversy. Irrespective of what did, or didn't, occur there in late 1980, the forest has reportedly been the setting for ongoing anomalous phenomena, including UFO sightings and poltergeist-type manifestations.

SOURCES

A number of people have provided me with accounts of unusual experiences that they've had in or near the forest. I've also drawn on various written sources, principally the following books:

You Can't Tell the People by Georgina Bruni
UFOs & Nukes by Robert Hastings
The Rendlesham File by Andrew Pike

Pike's book is massive (over 750 pages) and very detailed, but it lacks an index, which it very much needs. The punctuation makes it difficult to follow in places; and, in my view, the book isn't as well structured as it could have been. Helpfully, though, on pp. 677–705, he presents a timeline of what he thinks most likely occurred in late December 1980.

THE AREA

Rendlesham Forest lies to the east of Woodbridge, close to the North Sea coast, and is predominantly coniferous. It was planted by the Forestry Commission, between 1922 and the late 1930s, on comparatively flat terrain that was formerly heath or agricultural land. It's criss-crossed by tracks, firebreaks and roads. The 1:25,000 (2½in to 1 mile) Ordnance Survey map no. 212 (*Woodbridge & Saxmunden*) depicts the area. The term 'Track 10' appears in this chapter. I've used inverted commas, because the track isn't currently marked with a number. At least, it wasn't when I visited the area in 2007 and in 2018. But people interested in UFO-related matters continue to refer to it as 'Track 10'. Its location is shown on the map opposite.

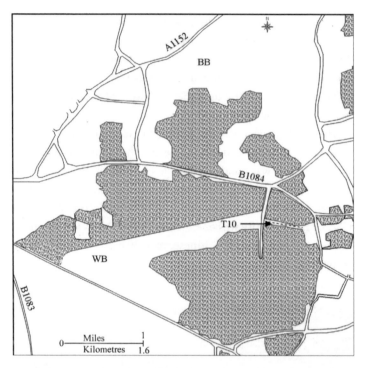

Rendlesham Forest (WB = Woodbridge base; BB = site of Bentwaters base; T10 = 'Track 10').

To the north of the forest is the site of a former air force base, RAF Bentwaters. The forest itself is largely bisected by the runway of another former air force base, RAF Woodbridge. In 1951, the United States Air Force (USAF) started taking over RAF Bentwaters, and within a couple of years they also took over the lease of RAF Woodbridge. Then, as now, the UK and USA were members of the North Atlantic Treaty Organization (NATO), a military alliance. Bentwaters was officially closed in 1993, following the end of the Cold War, and the USAF also left the Woodbridge installation that year.

Since September 2006, the Woodbridge site has been officially known as MoD Woodbridge. It's now used by the British Army's 23 Parachute Engineer Regiment, which provides support to the 16 Air Assault Brigade, a rapid reaction force. The Army Air Corps periodically uses the airfield for training exercises involving helicopters.

The Suffolk coast was the setting for secret military-related activity for several decades in the twentieth century. For example, radar research was conducted at Orford Ness in the mid-1930s and then transferred to Bawdsey Manor (renamed as Bawdsey Research Station) in Felixstowe; and from 1967 to 1973, a joint US/UK radar facility was operated at Orford Ness, to help monitor Soviet, and possibly Chinese, missile tests, satellite vehicle launchings and aircraft movements.

Looking east along 'Track 10'.

THE TWIN BASES IN DECEMBER 1980

The most senior USAF officer at the Bentwaters and Woodbridge bases at the time of the RFI was Colonel Gordon E. Williams of the 81st Tactical Fighter Wing. He had the functional title 'Wing Commander', which shouldn't be confused with the RAF rank of Wing Commander. Although the bases were geographically separated by Rendlesham Forest, they operated under a unified command structure. The Vice Wing Commander was Brian Currie. Below the 'Wing', the highest echelon of the command structure, there were four commanders, one for each of the four major departments: Operations; Maintenance; Rescue Management; Combat Support Group. Georgina Bruni explains that the Combat Support Group's remit was basically to manage the housekeeping and deal with security and policing.[1] It was headed by Colonel Ted Conrad, whose deputy was Lieutenant Colonel Charles I. Halt. The latter played a prominent role in the RFI. Conrad had the functional title of 'Base Commander', and Halt was known as the 'Deputy Base Commander'. But these are confusing designations, since they could lead one to think that Conrad and Halt were the two most senior officers at the twin bases. (The USAF eventually stopped referring to Combat Support Group commanders as 'Base Commanders'.)

The RFI occurred during a tense time in the Cold War. Georgina Bruni explains that A-10 'tank buster' aircraft were deployed at Bentwaters in 1979,[2] and that a reliable military source had informed her that then super-secret stealth F-117 aircraft were deployed there in the early 1980s.[3] She notes that the 67th Aerospace Rescue and Recovery Squadron transferred from Spain to RAF Woodbridge in 1969.[4] They were primarily trained for recovering space vehicles that had splashed down in the Atlantic and Indian Oceans. But following cutbacks by the National Aeronautical and Space Agency (NASA), and the ending of the lunar missions, they concentrated on air rescues behind enemy lines. Additionally, they were known, and praised, for rescuing civilians.

INCIDENTS PRIOR TO THE RFI

STRANGE LIGHTS AND UFOS

Strange lights were allegedly seen in the Rendlesham area during the late 1800s.[5] In the twentieth century, there were reportedly sightings of lights or UFOs prior to the controversial events of December 1980. For example, Georgina Bruni cites a witness called F.W. Sone, who'd been a security policeman (within the USAF, presumably) at the Bentwaters base.[6] Around 3 a.m. one day in 1973, he allegedly saw a light hovering over the main runway. Shortly after, spotlights from fire/rescue trucks were trained on the silent, hovering light, which appeared to be about 100 feet in diameter. After about five minutes, it suddenly disappeared. The following year, while on duty in the weapons storage area of the base, Sone reportedly witnessed an incident in which two F-4 fighters were sent to intercept a UFO. But as they approached the object, it became smaller and suddenly disappeared, only to reappear in another place. That allegedly went on for thirty minutes, the UFO seemingly playing games with the pilots. According to Sone, about twenty personnel witnessed the sighting.

GHOSTLY PHENOMENA AND STRANGE CREATURES

Georgina Bruni describes ghostly phenomena that were reportedly experienced by American air force personnel, although none of the accounts appears to have been given to her by a first-hand witness. James D. Hudnall, who'd been a USAF security guard at the

Bentwaters base in the mid 1970s, told her about some experiences that befell a colleague of his called Andy.[7] The latter was on duty in the weapons storage area one foggy, wintry night when he spotted three figures heading towards the security tower. A patrol vehicle was alerted and entered the area. But when its headlights shone on them, the figures disappeared. A search revealed nothing. Later that night, Andy heard footsteps ascending the metal steps of the tower, although he wasn't expecting visitors. When he opened the trapdoor and shone his torchlight down, he saw nothing. He closed the trapdoor and resumed his watch. But very soon after, he heard footsteps again, which were louder than before and getting closer and closer. Andy went for his gun and stood ready. The trapdoor swung wide open and then slammed shut, but there was nothing to be seen.

In an article about the Rendlesham Forest phenomena, Nick Redfern refers to a witness called Sam Holland, who'd reportedly had an unusual encounter while walking through the forest with his spaniel dog in early 1956.[8] He was horrified to see a bizarre-looking four-legged creature loom out of the trees about 40 feet ahead of him. Its legs were huge and muscular, it was easily 10 feet in length, and its thick fur was black and glossy. When the beast turned in his direction, Holland saw that it had a huge neck, widely flared nostrils, and immense, powerful-looking jaws. He likened its face to that of a silverback gorilla. The creature looked intently at Holland and his whimpering dog for a moment or two, and then went off into the surrounding undergrowth. Holland inferred, probably correctly, that this was a paranormal experience rather than an encounter with something physical in origin. Another person to have an unusual experience in the area was a motorist called Jimmy Freeman. He told Redfern that he was driving past Rendlesham Forest one dark, cloudy and slightly misty night in the 1970s when, in his full beam, he saw something large and shadowy charging across the road in front of him. He was convinced that it was a huge black cat.

LATE DECEMBER 1980 ('THE RFI')

January 1970 saw the closure of Project Blue Book, the USAF's last publicly admitted attempt to investigate UFO reports. Of course, whether the USAF actually stopped taking an interest in the UFO phenomenon might be questioned. At any rate, it seems that around the time of the RFI, there was an implicit understanding among USAF personnel that reporting UFO activity, or being associated with UFO reports, might attract unwelcome attention from within the air force (e.g. from the investigative branch known as the Air Force Office of Special Investigations), and could be inimical to one's military career. Certainly, Charles Halt feared that his being caught up in the RFI might not be 'career-enhancing'. But things didn't turn out too badly for him, since he was made a full colonel sometime after the RFI, perhaps because he was recommended for promotion before the case received massive publicity.

The events of December 1980 mainly involved the eastern part of the forest, where there's now an official 'UFO Trail' to commemorate the RFI. In a clearing close to the eastern edge of the forest, not far from the aforementioned 'Track 10', there's a sculptured UFO. Whether it's in the precise spot where a landed or hovering UFO was seen (see below), I'm not sure.

THE 'HALT MEMORANDUM' AND 'HALT TAPE'

The RFI largely involved USAF personnel. But because the main events occurred outside the twin bases themselves, the Americans could claim that it was a British responsibility and not something they needed to investigate. A couple of weeks after the RFI, Halt wrote a brief memorandum about the events for the British authorities, but it seemed to contain mistakes regarding dates.

The 'Halt Memorandum', as it became known, came to public light in 1983, thanks to ufologists in the USA making use of their country's Freedom of Information Act. It referred to 'a strange glowing object' that had been sighted in the forest early in the morning of 27 December 1980 (which we should probably take to have been the early morning of *26* December of that year). The object was described as metallic in appearance and triangular.[9] The document stated that, as patrolmen approached it, the object manoeuvred through the trees and disappeared but was seen again, briefly, about an hour later. The memorandum stated that indentations were later found where the object had been seen on the ground, and radiation was subsequently detected there. The memorandum went on to refer to further sightings, witnessed by numerous people (including Halt himself), on the night of 29/30 December (although these events probably occurred before then – on the night of 27/28 December). It claimed that:

- A sun-like light was seen through the trees, and moved about and pulsed. At one point, 'it appeared to throw off glowing particles and then broke into five separate white objects and then disappeared.'

- Immediately after this, three star-like objects were spotted in the sky, two to the north, and one to the south, all of them being about ten degrees off the horizon. They moved rapidly, with sharp, angular movements, and displayed red, green and blue lights.

- Viewed through an 8-12 power lens, the objects to the north seemed elliptical. They then became 'full circles'. They were in the sky for an hour or more.

- The object to the south was seen for two or three hours, and at times beamed down a stream of light.

The memorandum's portrayal of what supposedly occurred during those late December days is very limited. When Halt went into Rendlesham Forest on the night briefly described in the third paragraph of the memorandum, he had a Dictaphone with him, which he used to record comments about what was happening. Copies of the recording, and a transcript of it, later became widely available. (The transcript can be found, for example, in the books by Georgina Bruni and Andrew Pike.) However, Pike believes that the released tape was edited down, and that its contents may have been compiled from several tapes.[10] If so, the transcript will, of course, reflect that editing.

UNCERTAINTIES

Because of conflicting testimony from witnesses or alleged witnesses,[11] the fact that people have changed their stories, and uncertainty about dates and the precise timing of events, we'll probably never know for sure exactly what occurred during the RFI. There are claims that some of the USAF personnel were subjected to questioning or interrogation facilitated by drugs and hypnosis. If so, it's possible that their recollections were irretrievably erased or mutated, perhaps deliberately, with a view to covering up whatever happened. That's not beyond the realms of possibility, given the political and military context at the time. Furthermore, Pike's book refers to the long history of 'mind control' research carried out by, or on behalf of, organisations such as the Central Intelligence Agency (CIA).[12] He also notes that if witnesses' brains were being affected by electromagnetic activity at the time, it wouldn't be surprising that their recollections varied. For a detailed reconstruction of what *may have been* the course of events, I'd recommend Chapter 14 of his book.

SPECULATIONS

I'll mention, just briefly, some of the speculations that have been offered to account for what supposedly happened during the RFI.

Hard-line sceptics (referred to as *debunkers* by Andrew Pike) have suggested that USAF personnel mistook the flashing beacon of the Orford Ness lighthouse, to the east of the forest, for a mysterious object. But the 'lighthouse theory' faces multiple problems. For example, around midnight on the night of 25/26 December 1980, airmen at the East Gate of the Woodbridge base saw strange lights in Rendlesham Forest. But the beacon of the Orford Ness lighthouse couldn't be seen from that location.

The East Gate.

Brenda Butler, Dot Street and Jenny Randles, the authors of the first book about the RFI, considered the possibility that something mundane had occurred, which the authorities wanted to conceal from public attention, and that a UFO story was concocted to cover up what had happened. But, as they noted, that would have almost guaranteed that attention would be drawn to the area.[13]

Georgina Bruni (2001, pp. 363–64) argued that it could no longer be disputed that a craft of unknown origin landed in the forest,[14] and she concluded that time-travellers from our future, or beings from 'another dimension', were involved.[15]

In his book, which draws heavily on science, Andrew Pike considers a wide range of possibilities. For example, naturally or artificially induced electromagnetic effects may have affected the perception and memory of witnesses, and secret military drones may have generated local UFO sightings.

INCIDENTS SINCE DECEMBER 1980

UFO SIGHTINGS

Charles Halt informed researcher Robert Hastings that on the night of 5 November 1981, two security police patrols saw a large cigar-shaped object that floated in from the direction of the sea and looped around the Woodbridge tower.[16] And James Burris, a former USAF security policeman, informed Hastings about a sighting that he and two colleagues had had around November 1982. They reportedly saw three sets of lights hanging over Rendlesham Forest. During the sighting, a truck that Burris and two other servicemen were travelling in temporarily broke down.[17]

Georgina Bruni also mentions UFO sightings that postdate the RFI. For example, she mentions an Ipswich couple who saw a 'huge spaceship' (Bruni's words) one evening in 1996, the sighting occurring between Woodbridge and the village of Eyke.[18]

A SPECTRAL DOG WITH FELINE CHARACTERISTICS

The aforementioned article by Nick Redfern (referenced in Note 8) mentions an experience that befell a couple called Paul and Jane on a winter's afternoon in 1983 when they were walking along a pathway in Rendlesham Forest. (It's not clear from Redfern's wording whether the incident occurred in early 1983 or at the end of the year, both of which would have been winter.) Rounding a bend, they came face to face with a strange creature. Its head was reportedly canine in appearance, but much larger than that of any normal dog, although its body seemed to have feline characteristics. There appeared to be an eerily mournful expression on its face. In the words of one of the witnesses, the creature began to 'flicker on and off'. That happened four or five times, and then it vanished before their eyes. At the same time, there was an overwhelming smell that reminded the couple of burning metal. They fled to their car and quickly left the area.

PERSONAL ENQUIRIES

During a visit to the locality in March 2007, I met several people who claimed to have had unusual experiences in Rendlesham Forest; and I was subsequently in touch with other witnesses. I was mainly interested in recent or ongoing phenomena rather than the RFI.

I've given the real names of my informants, except where indicated. For ease of expression, I'll be sparing in the use of distancing terminology ('alleged', 'reportedly', etc.). I can't guarantee the historical accuracy of what I've been told, although I've no reason to believe that any of the informants lied to me. The witnesses I cite aren't the only people who claim to have had unusual experiences in the forest. Three people who said they'd provide me with written accounts of their experiences failed to do so; and, for all I know, there could be many others who have had strange experiences in the area.

The recollections reported under each of the following sub-headings are those of the person named in the subheading and not necessarily those of any other person mentioned.

BRENDA BUTLER

Brenda Butler, a former nurse, was (and perhaps still is) living near the Suffolk coast. She declined to divulge her age, but she reported a long history of unusual experiences. She told me that her first UFO sighting occurred when she was 5. She believed that she'd been abducted by aliens on several occasions, and she said that she played with aliens when she was a child. She told me that she had three scars that she believed might have been related to her contact with aliens, and she told me that she'd spoken in a weird language at times. She informed me that someone had turned up on her doorstep in 1984, had stayed for three months, and had subsequently returned for a further week. The visitor slept in a nearby caravan rather than in her house. He usually appeared in human form. But on three occasions, she'd seen him as a 'Reptilian' (an alien with reptilian features). She told me that he'd been able to discern her thoughts telepathically, that he knew what was in books without having to read them, and that he sometimes appeared unexpectedly before her. He ate only vegetables and sweets, and didn't appear to wash or use the lavatory, although he always looked clean.

Butler had been visiting Rendlesham Forest since 1979, and she regarded it as a very magical place. But she had doubts about whether the RFI involved anything exotic, although she believed that extraterrestrials and beings from another dimension were involved in the ongoing phenomena. She'd taken numerous photographs in the forest, initially using 35 mm film and then digital cameras. Many of the photographs had been taken at night. 'Orbs', misty patches and streaks of light or colour could be seen in many of them. Generally, those features hadn't been evident to the naked eye when the photographs were taken. In addition, she reported having had numerous unusual experiences in the forest over the years, including: sightings of UFOs and apparitions (e.g. of small monk-like figures); missing time; her watch stopping; hot or warm stones dropping down beside her; and her surroundings appearing temporarily different from normal.

Many of the experiences had occurred when she'd been in company. For example, she reported that during a visit to the forest in about 1998, she and an American, called Woody, saw a helicopter chasing a large white light. Two smaller lights came out of the larger light and then went back into it. Other strange things occurred. For example, the couple experienced a few hours of missing time, and, for a while, the local topography appeared to be different from normal. On another occasion, in the same general area (the eastern part of the forest), she noticed a 6-foot tree at a spot where there'd been no tree about a week before. But when she returned, about ten days later, the tree wasn't there!

PETER PARISH

Peter Parish was about 48 when I met him in 2007, and he was working as a groundsman at a school. He recalled childhood experiences of feeling pinned down in his bedroom and feeling as if he were being visited, although he didn't actually see any 'visitors'. (These may have been episodes of what's known as *sleep paralysis*.) Some years prior to my meeting him, he'd had a similar experience at Brenda Butler's home, although on that occasion he subsequently saw, or hallucinated, a rotating blob of fluorescent green material that resembled antifreeze liquid. The sighting seemed to last about twenty to thirty seconds. (Butler informed me that other people had had apparitional experiences at her home.)

Using a DVD camcorder and a digital camera, Parish had captured moving images in the forest of what he and Brenda Butler called 'rods'. Seeing them on DVD, I thought their shape was reminiscent of pictures of the DNA molecule. I wasn't sure what to make of them, but I wondered whether they could have been photographic artefacts or images of airborne bracken fibres. Interestingly, Parish thought that rods were more in evidence when the bracken was high in the forest.

One evening in January 2002, while he was living in a flat that was formerly part of RAF Bentwaters, Parish saw an army helicopter flying very low over the flats, seemingly chasing, or being passed by, a bluish-white orb-shaped light that was heading east. And in about 2002, from Woodbridge, he saw a Sea King helicopter being followed by an orb of light. Of course, these may have been observations of modern-day (albeit, perhaps, secret) military technology and not anything exotic or paranormal.

Parish had had UFO experiences in Rendlesham Forest itself. One windless, starlit night, some years prior to our meeting, he was looking down 'Track 10' from the road that runs past its western end when he and Brenda Butler heard a whirring noise, as if some sort of craft were flying towards them from the trees ahead. There was a bright flash in the forest, and then the noise resumed and came closer. They felt wind swirling around them and noticed the trees swaying. Nothing was visible, and the noise moved away in the direction of the Woodbridge base. However, a possible explanation is that a military helicopter was on a night-flying exercise.

On another occasion, during the daytime, Parish saw a light-brown object shoot up from 'Track 10' into a tree. It appeared to be about 20 to 30 inches long, 4 inches wide, and resembled a stick of French bread.

Parish informed me that very warm stones had sometimes landed beside him in the forest. That had happened during the day, and also at night, in warm weather; and he'd experienced the phenomenon both on his own and with others. He stated that for the phenomenon to occur in the presence of a group of people, the group had to be reasonably small, and its members had to be open-minded. He explained that the stones were always smooth, and he'd sometimes seen them before they'd hit the ground. In his experience, they landed without bouncing, although if they were picked up and then dropped, they would bounce normally. At one point, an elongated stone landed on its end in his presence; and one evening, while his car was parked near 'Track 10', a stone landed on its roof, without rolling off.

Standing alone at the western end of 'Track 10' one night, Parish asked, out loud, 'Are you from another dimension?' A stone then fell down beside him. He asked, 'Can you drop a stone on the track in front of me where I'm shining the torch beam?' That duly happened. And when he asked whether a stone could be dropped on the road behind him, one obligingly fell there!

On maybe two or three occasions, Parish had been among quite densely spaced trees in the eastern part of the forest when a stone had landed near his feet – but without there being a preceding sound of something falling through the branches overhead. At one point, he was on 'Track 10' when a stone landed on the ground between his legs. He had a rucksack on his back at the time, so it's hard to see how the stone could have come from above.

In the company of Brenda Butler, Parish had sometimes experienced brief visions of small monk-like creatures. But these sightings had occurred less often than the incidents involving falling stones. One night in April 2002, he was with Butler and some other people near 'Track 10' when he saw a human-shaped shadow passing him, going to the left. At first, he mistakenly took it to be one of his companions, John Hanson. The figure walked over a deep hole in a path in front of Parish, without falling over. And after that, he and Butler saw a round light moving about in a nearby birch tree.

At one point, some symbols came into Parish's mind while he was meditating in the eastern part of the forest. He was in the forest two or three days later when he got a 'message' (mental impression) telling him that something was on the left, not very far away. Some three days later, he and Brenda Butler were in that part of the forest and came upon a stone on which some of the self-same symbols had been scratched.

There was an occasion when, after meditating with Brenda Butler in the eastern part of the forest, Parish discovered that two and a half hours had passed, although it had only seemed like half an hour to him.

VALERIE WILSON (PSEUDONYM)

Valerie Wilson was about 38 when I met and corresponded with her in 2007. She hails from London but now lives in Suffolk. Like Brenda Butler, she reports a long history of anomalous experiences.

When she was 6, she had an out-of-body experience. She saw three humanoids in her bedroom when she was 11. She'd seen UFOs over her home, and she'd experienced phenomena within it, such as sightings of 'Reptilians' and 'Greys'. She explained that for many years, she'd experienced electrical disturbances. She stated:

> I touch the switch to turn on lights and fuse the whole house. I do this at friends' homes. Street lights flicker or switch on or off when I approach them or walk under them. I leave the doctor's room to allow them to get my details up on the screen as their computer crashes in my presence. I give static shocks to people when they get in my car ....

Wilson explained that her partner had also experienced unusual phenomena. For example, when they lived in London, he saw a blue globe of light appear in the centre of their kitchen. And she reported that all three of her children had experienced paranormal activity.

Given that so many unusual things had happened to her elsewhere, it's perhaps not surprising to learn that Wilson had also experienced phenomena in Rendlesham Forest. One night in about August 2006, while she was sitting in her car in a picnic area next to a campsite in the forest, an entity, about 2½ to 3 feet tall, fell on to the bonnet! Startled, she dived into the back of the car. The entity remained on the bonnet for two or three minutes. On another occasion, around 11.30 p.m., while she was sitting on a bench near 'Track 10' with some companions, she turned on a tape-recorder. When the tape was played back, clicking sounds could be heard. But she hadn't heard them while the recording was being made. On a couple of occasions, she saw red lights high in some trees near the B1084 road. During another visit to the forest, she heard a noise like the satisfied purr of a big cat.

LAURA (PSEUDONYM)

Laura, whom I spoke to on the phone in 2007, was then about 16. She told me that she was with her mother and their dog in Rendlesham Forest, probably just before Christmas 2006, when a stone rolled along the ground near them. Her mother picked it up, and it was burning hot. From Laura's description, I think they were probably on 'Track 10' at the time.

JOHN HANSON

John Hanson was about 61 when I was first in touch with him, in 2007. He's a retired police officer with an interest in UFO phenomena. He and Dawn Holloway (see below) have co-authored a series of books on British UFO cases (the *Haunted Skies* series). Hanson and Holloway had made repeated visits to Rendlesham Forest. He informed me that he'd seen 'orbs' there. In the company of others, he and Holloway had sometimes been in the forest at night when a thud had been heard, followed by the discovery, on the ground beside them, of a smooth, rounded and hot pebble. At one point, he was struck lightly on the back by a stone in the forest.

DAWN HOLLOWAY

Dawn Holloway was about 52 when I contacted her in 2007. There was an occasion when, using a non-digital camera, she photographed an 'orb' in daylight conditions in Rendlesham Forest, although she hadn't seen anything strange at the time. At that stage, she and Hanson weren't observing the anomalous things that their friend Brenda Butler reported seeing. On another occasion, Butler asked them whether they could see light around a tree. At first, neither of them could, but then it seemed to Holloway that the tree was shimmering with light, although Hanson still couldn't see it. On their next visit to the forest, Holloway saw what looked like a light in a tree close to a track. Butler indicated that she could also see it, although it wasn't evident to Hanson and the other people present. According to Holloway, as Hanson looked more intently, he then saw it, and it showed up in a photograph that he took. Holloway stated that after that visit, she and Hanson began to see 'orbs' with the naked eye, and that Hanson captured a great deal with his digital camera. Holloway confirmed that stones had sometimes landed on the ground when she'd been in the forest. She described them as having been 'quite warm'.

DON RAMKIN

Don Ramkin was about 45 when I was in touch with him, in 2007. He'd had a longstanding interest in the paranormal and had been visiting Rendlesham Forest for several years. During his initial visits, he neither saw nor photographed anything unusual. But after that, he had a variety of unusual experiences, and captured anomalous photographic images. He tended to visit the forest as part of a foursome, including Brenda Butler, and he informed me that he and Butler had concluded that unusual activity was more likely to occur if there were just four of them.

Ramkin reported having seen anomalous lights or illuminated objects in the forest. One incident occurred when he was walking down a track at night with several others. He and John Hanson were at the rear, walking parallel to each other, some distance apart, and chatting. An object resembling a bright golf ball shot out of the trees ahead of them on the left, at an angle. Ramkin noted: '[I]t … zipped between myself and John … just above our heads, seemed to twist, [and] then, taking another trajectory, shot into the trees to the right, behind us.' It made a rasping-like noise.

Judging from its high-speed manoeuvres, Ramkin inferred that it was being guided or had intelligence. (I spoke to John Hanson about the incident, but he didn't have a specific recollection of it. If it happened as described, it may be that he wasn't looking in the right direction at the time.)

Ramkin mentioned an occasion when he saw a silent, black, tri-angular-shaped craft flying in the direction of Orford Ness, about half an hour before it got fully dark. It appeared to be at a high altitude and above a field rather than over the forest itself. He'd had other unusual visual experiences in the area, including sightings of apparitional figures. He reported that he and his companions had had their clothing tugged, and that they'd been prodded; and he related that he distinctly felt someone, or something, unseen holding his right hand on two occasions. And on three occasions, he felt a grip around his left wrist. (If I understood him correctly, all of these incidents involving tactile impressions occurred at night.)

One night, Ramkin and two companions, including Brenda Butler, were sitting on a bench near 'Track 10' when he heard someone whispering in his right ear. He asked Butler what she'd said, but then realised that there was no one sitting to his right. Butler explained that no one had spoken. Ramkin then heard more whispering.

Ramkin informed me that he'd been present when stones had fallen in the forest. Usually, they'd landed near him and his companions, and, if located, had been very warm. He noted that they could be pure white and almost polished, unlike the stones that he and his companions had normally come across in the forest. He reported that he'd personally witnessed two stones land and roll; and he also mentioned an occasion when a plastic toy elephant landed at the base of a tree.

One night, Ramkin and a companion were walking down a forest track when they heard a loud rushing and crashing sound from some trees to their right. In his torchlight, Ramkin saw a deer running fast. It fell but got up and ran off. He panned his torch around and suddenly saw two pairs of yellow eyes looking back at him and his companion. At first, the men thought they were seeing foxes. As Ramkin and his companion walked on, the two creatures walked on, and when the men stopped, the creatures stopped. But Ramkin's torchlight kept illuminating the creatures' eyes, so he knew where they were. When he caught a glimpse of shoulder blades going up and down, he inferred that the creatures were big cats.

COMMENTS

Without reliable comparative data, it's hard to know for sure whether Rendlesham Forest is a hotbed of strange events. If a randomly selected area of a similar size, population and land cover were closely studied, perhaps just as many strange incidents would come to light. However, in the light of what we know, I think there's at least a *prima facie* case for thinking that the forest has hosted a disproportionate number of odd occurrences.

There's much controversy about what happened in the forest in late December 1980, and I shan't comment further on it, except to note that people may be missing an important part of the picture by focusing on such a brief period. I suspect that this narrow focus is because many commentators are primarily concerned with UFO phenomena, or with trying to explain away such phenomena, and that they have relatively little interest in the broader subject of the paranormal. Regarding what happened before 1980, there's nothing more that I can usefully add. I'll therefore focus my discussion on the testimony that I've cited about more recent events.

PSYCHOLOGICAL FACTORS

A desire to experience unusual phenomena no doubt attracts people to Rendlesham Forest. In some cases, experiences may be shaped by expectation, suggestion and imagination. In respect of nocturnal visits, darkness and sleep deprivation could be conducive to perceptual errors. Furthermore, if incidents aren't noted down very soon after they've occurred, they could be recalled inaccurately. (Regarding events involving more than one witness, I noticed two or three discrepancies in the testimony of my informants. But generally speaking, there was a fair amount of consensus.)

Some people might be especially prone to perceptual errors and to misjudging the passage of time. Someone with a marked tendency to become very focused on one particular thing, to the exclusion of everything else, might lose track of time in certain situations. And someone with a predisposition to confuse internally generated imagery with external perceptions might be particularly susceptible to hallucinations in a forest at night. Furthermore, if sights and sounds are ambiguous, as they might well be in the dark of night, a person's interpretation of them could be influenced by the pronouncements of companions – if the peer group deems that an ambiguous event was paranormal, that might induce a waverer to interpret it that way.

However, these are notes of caution, and this case includes physical manifestations that can't be convincingly explained away in purely psychological terms.

FALLING STONES

Incidents involving hot or warm stones feature in the testimony of several witnesses. A sceptic might conjecture that one of them used trickery to fabricate the incidents. However, it appears that none of the witnesses was consistently present each time the manifestation occurred. For example, Peter Parish reported having experienced it on his own, and Brenda Butler told me that it had occurred in his absence. In itself, that doesn't entirely rule out trickery, although I rather doubt whether the incidents arose from hoaxing, not least because the perpetrator(s) would have had to spend a considerable amount of time carrying out the pranks. Equally, I think it's unlikely that my informants conspired to lie to me. Indeed, since 2007, I've heard of other people experiencing the falling-stone phenomenon in the forest. For example, a Ronnie Dugdale informed me that it had happened to him, although he couldn't recall the date.

The falling of hot or warm stones has been reported in some poltergeist-type cases – for example, on Canvey Island, Essex, in 1709.[19] Poltergeist phenomena often revolve around a particular person. But, as indicated above, the stone-falling incidents in Rendlesham Forest haven't been consistently linked with any particular person. Accordingly, they may have been place-linked phenomena. However, in 2007, Nigel Turner, the Recreation Ranger at Rendlesham Forest, informed me that he wasn't aware of any of the forestry workers having such experiences with stones. Therefore, these incidents may be infrequent.

THE PHOTOGRAPHIC EVIDENCE

Brenda Butler kindly gave me a CD containing a large number of photographs that she'd taken in Rendlesham Forest. Many of them showed 'orbs' and other anomalies. I sought an opinion about some of the images from a professional photographer. In the main, he thought that the abnormalities could be accounted for in prosaic terms, such as 'camera shake' and 'colour noise'.

However, there was no evidence of sophisticated image-processing software being used to produce the effects, and I have no reason to think that Butler faked any photographs.

By way of an informal control experiment, I took some digital photographs at night in two wooded locations not far from my home. Although I didn't see anything unusual at the time, the camera recorded some 'orbs' at one of the sites. These were presumably normal artefacts, and I suspect that many of the apparent photographic anomalies recorded in Rendlesham Forest are of a similar nature.

However, it might be wrong to conclude that there's no mystery at all about the photographic images obtained in the forest. Writing to me in 2007, Don Ramkin noted:

> [When] I first started going [there] and was taking endless photos and not getting a single thing, I complained that my camera was crap and that I'd wasted my money buying it. So Brenda [Butler], who was getting orbs and streakers, said, 'Let me try.'

According to Ramkin, she took a photograph with his camera, and straight away two 'orbs' appeared in the frame. Once Ramkin had 'become tuned in with the forest', as he put it, he found himself getting everything he hoped for and more. He wrote: 'Since then, we've had people with us who have expensive cameras … and get nothing, and I've asked to try, [and have] taken a photo with their equipment and got orbs, mist, etc.' He explained that when he was in the forest, he would sometimes experience a headache feeling across his forehead, and that at such times, 'I guarantee that if we [took] photos, there [would] be orbs or mist.'

WHAT'S BEHIND THE PHENOMENA?

If some of the manifestations are paranormal, what lies behind them? Could it be that people's minds, interacting at a subconscious level, are capable of generating paranormal phenomena, including UFO sightings? Applying this notion to Rendlesham Forest, one might conjecture that many of the manifestations have been created, unwittingly, by people with a strong interest in the local phenomena, and particularly by those who visit the forest in the hope of having unusual experiences. Their situation could be compared to that of people who regularly attend séances. If there's some truth in this notion, it may be that certain participants play a more prominent role than others in unconsciously catalysing or generating phenomena. Brenda Butler may fall into that category. As noted, she reports having had a good number of paranormal experiences in her life, and she's been a very frequent visitor to Rendlesham Forest over the years.

Another possibility is that there's some sort of external intelligence (not necessarily extraterrestrial) behind the Rendlesham Forest phenomena. It may have the capacity to produce a wide range of effects, involving both objective and hallucinatory manifestations.

9

BRIEFER REPORTS

This chapter includes a selection of reports from across Britain, not all of which involve named witnesses. Obviously, the anonymous accounts warrant particular caution.

GLASGOW, SCOTLAND

GARTLOCH HOSPITAL

Gartloch Hospital, on the eastern fringe of Glasgow, was principally a psychiatric hospital. It received its first patients in 1896, and it closed in 1996. Some eighteen years ago, a couple of women told me of ghostly experiences that they'd had while working there. One of them had reportedly had multiple spooky experiences during her time there as a nurse. For example, she related that approximately twenty years previously, while staying at the nurses' home, she would hear children singing outside around 10 or 11 p.m., and that the sounds seemed to come from some nearby woods. As she recalled, this happened in the wintertime. More recently, she'd been told about someone hearing children singing 'Ring a Ring o' Roses' at the back of the nurses' home.

This is reminiscent of something that allegedly happened during the construction of the Stocksbridge bypass (A616) in South Yorkshire in the 1980s. Author David Clarke quotes a John Holmes, who'd worked in a lorry depot immediately below the new road during its construction. He stated that he and fellow workers had a strong feeling that they were being watched, and that they often heard children singing late at night. The sounds seemed to come from some woods.[1]

NORTHUMBERLAND

BOLAM LAKE COUNTRY PARK

Bolam Lake Country Park is located about 9 miles west of Morpeth. The lake itself is surrounded by woods. The park covers an area of some 65 acres. In his book *Man-Monkey* (pp. 121–26), Nick Redfern explains that members of the Devon-based Centre for Fortean Zoology (CFZ) visited the area in January 2003, to investigate reports of a bigfoot-like entity being seen there.[2] The following are a few examples of what they were told and experienced during their investigation.

At one point, the CFZ team discovered that nearly all of their electronic equipment was suffering from a loss of power, even though they'd tested their items the previous night and had charged-up or replaced batteries where necessary.

The team interviewed a mother and her son who'd sighted a huge creature at the park only days before. It had stood motionless in the woods near the car park, which the witnesses were crossing at the time. They'd felt intense fear and had quickly left the area. Another witness, Neil, had several experiences to relate. For example, he mentioned an occasion, a couple of summers previously, when he and his girlfriend were having sex in the woods at the park. His girlfriend saw what she took to be a man in a monkey suit, watching them from behind a bush. Neil looked around the area but couldn't find anything.

On the afternoon of the second day of their investigation, the CFZ team liaised with members of a local investigative group called Twilight Worlds (TW). Around 5 p.m., with the help of car headlights, five of them saw an enormous man-shaped figure run from right to left. It disappeared for a few moments, and then ran back again.

Of course, one might wonder whether at least some of the local bigfoot sightings were generated by hoaxers. Nick Redfern explains that an article in the local press in February 2003 mentioned that two sixth-formers at Gosforth High School had roamed about in a hired gorilla costume in Kielder Forest in the summer of 2002, this being part of an arts project at their school.[3] However, Redfern states that Kielder Forest is more than 40 miles from Bolam Lake (in fact, it's about 25 miles away, as the crow flies), and that the sixth-formers were adamant that none of their activities had occurred at Bolam Lake. He states that the school is only 7 miles from Bolam Lake (again, though, he seems to have got the distance wrong – it's further than that). He speculates that maybe someone else – possibly another student at the school – secretly hired the same gorilla costume and paraded about in it at Bolam Lake.

But irrespective of whether some of the earlier sightings were hoaxed, Redfern suggests that what the CFZ and TW members observed in January 2003 was a 'thought-form', a paranormal manifestation born out of belief and expectation.[4] He contends that the encounter couldn't, under any circumstances, be blamed on the antics of a student at the school, particularly given the utterly 'flat', huge and shadow-like nature of what was seen.

WEST YORKSHIRE

JUDY WOODS, NEAR BRADFORD

Between Bradford and Brighouse, there's a small complex of woodland known as Judy Woods. In his book *Earth Lights Revelation*, Paul Devereux notes that the woodland lies near a reservoir and power lines, and that it was the setting for a small UFO flap in the autumn of 1981 (p. 105).[5] Initially, bright streaks of light, similar to lightning, were seen. Then, over a period of weeks, lights were seen flashing and hovering above the woods. Blobs of light appeared. They split into smaller pieces, which hovered and floated down. Humming sounds and odours (resembling that of rotten eggs) reportedly accompanied some of the sightings.

SOUTH YORKSHIRE

HAUNTED WOODLAND NEAR STOCKSBRIDGE

Jenny Randles relates a story, told to her by a Jane Hayes (pseudonym), about an incident in 1948.[6] Along with three others, Hayes was camping in a small wood, known locally as 'Spooky Woods'. (I think this refers to the wooded area on the north side of Broomhead Reservoir.) They were in their tent when they heard what sounded like a horse galloping towards them. But the noise stopped when it reached the tent. When they went out to look, there were no hoofmarks in the soft earth. Subsequently, Hayes was told by local farmers that they'd often seen lights in the wood, only to find nothing there when they went to investigate. Some ten years after she heard the ghostly galloping sounds, Hayes and her young son saw a circle of lights hovering over a reservoir behind the woods. This seems to be a reference to Broomhead Reservoir, which is about a mile south-south-west of Stocksbridge. The lights winked out, but Randles doesn't say for how long they were in view.

DERBYSHIRE

BUXTON COUNTRY PARK

At a conference I attended in October 2018, one of the speakers, Brian Sterling-Vete, referred to strange lights that he'd seen in a wooded area near the spa town of Buxton many years before. He's kindly sent me further information about his experiences. The woodland in question is to the south-west of the town centre, and not far from Solomon's Temple, a tower that crowns a high point to the south of Buxton.[7]

While making evening and late-night trips in and around the area in the late 1970s, Sterling-Vete noticed strange lights in the woodland of Buxton Country Park. Initially, he didn't give them much thought. Eventually, though, he asked some of the older locals about them. Their response, more or less, was to warn him off from becoming too curious about the lights, and certainly not to venture into the area where they were at night. It was almost as if they'd become irrationally superstitious –

unless, of course, they knew something fearful that they didn't want to admit to. Some people even spoke of witchcraft and of local covens using the area for rituals after dark. Again, Sterling-Vete would be cautioned to forget what he'd seen. But he wasn't disposed to take such advice. The next time he saw the lights, he stopped his car and went to investigate them, accompanied by a friend called Cliff Twemlow. They walked towards the woods without lighting a torch, which would have given away their presence. The lights were among the trees, but not above them. As the men got much closer, they still couldn't clearly discern what the lights were. But curiously, they seemed to be more like an aurora.

When Sterling-Vete and his friend arrived at the treeline, the lights were still ahead, but they suddenly dispersed as the men walked on. The witnesses then found themselves surrounded by lights, which seemed to be under intelligent control and trying to usher them out of the area. They had a strong sense that they were being watched by hundreds of eyes. Before long, they left the woods, never to return.

THE 'PHANTOM HELICOPTER'

In the early to mid-1970s, there were sightings of an unidentified 'helicopter' in northern England and the north Midlands. The appearances weren't specifically associated with wooded parts, but I'll mention them here, because some of them occurred close to the area mentioned by Brian Sterling-Vete. I've placed *helicopter* in inverted commas, because it's not clear whether the sightings were actually generated by one. Jenny Randles noted that 'helicopter' was an interpretation put on the reports by the local police and the media rather than by the witnesses themselves, who didn't usually describe what they saw as a helicopter.[8] If the sightings were indeed generated by a helicopter, its pilot must have been highly accomplished or foolhardy – or perhaps both – because it was seen flying at night, and close to the ground. Of course, it may be that more than one craft was flying over the area.

The period in question was a tense one for the UK, as there was much terrorist activity by Irish republicans. For example, in February 1972, the Official IRA planted a car bomb near the officers' mess of the 16th Parachute Brigade in Aldershot. Five female mess staff, a gardener, and a Roman Catholic padre were killed. Nineteen others were injured. And in February 1974, a bomb planted on a coach by the Provisional IRA killed nine soldiers and three civilians travelling on the M62 motorway in northern England. It was conjectured that the 'phantom helicopter' sightings were linked with activity by Irish republicans, or that a helicopter was being used for drug smuggling, or for bringing illegal immigrants into the country.

As noted, some of the sightings were in the Buxton area. At 1 a.m. on 18 September 1973, a resident at Harpur Hill, southeast of the town, saw what she thought was a helicopter rising out of Hillhead Quarry. She reported the matter to a security guard, Simon Crowe, who had some sightings of his own. In 1988, he informed David Clarke and Andy Roberts that his two 'best sightings' had been at the quarry at night. He stated that at no time did he positively identify the object as a helicopter, 'apart from its ability to hover and the sound from the rotor blades'. On the first occasion, the object hovered about 50 feet above the ground, shining spotlights downwards. When Crowe drove towards it, the object slowly rose and flew away. On the second occasion, it rose out of the quarry, and he wasn't aware of it until he saw its lights. It quickly disappeared in the same direction as previously.[9]

On 24 October 1975, a couple driving in a car encountered a flying object at Buxton. It came so low that it nearly hit them.

They plainly saw two rows of windows, separated by a bar. There were flashing red, green and white lights below the windows, and there was a faint humming sound. The object seemed to be as large as a bus at close quarters. At the same time, a witness in Cowdale, south-east of Buxton, also saw the object, which travelled low across the moors and passed over him.[10]

STAFFORDSHIRE

BAGOT'S WOOD, NEAR ABBOTS BROMLEY

In *The Monster Book* (pp. 307–09), Nick Redfern describes an experience that a 10-year-old boy, Alfred Tipton, allegedly had in the summer of 1937 with four friends in Bagot's Wood, which some spell without an apostrophe. (It's also known as 'Bagot's Forest' or 'Bagots Forest'.) It's located to the north of Abbot's Bromley, a few miles north-east of Cannock Chase. The wood is a remnant of what was once a much larger area of woodland, Needwood Forest.

After playing for several hours, Tipton and his friends were taking a break, sitting on the warm, dry grass in the sun, when they suddenly heard a shrill screeching sound coming from the trees above them. Looking up, they saw a large black creature sitting on its haunches in a particularly tall and very old tree. With its claws tightened around a branch, it was shaking it up and down. According to Tipton, it reminded him of a devil. It peered down at the five friends for a few moments and then suddenly opened up its large shiny wings. Their span was easily 12 feet. The creature took to the air in a way that could be described as a mixture of flying and gliding, and it was out of sight in what may have been fifteen to twenty seconds or so. Tipton was subsequently shown pictures, photographs and drawings of a wide variety of large-winged creatures from the present day and the past. The creature that most resembled what he and his friends had seen was a pterodactyl, an extinct flying reptile.

Redfern's discussion of the case can also be found on the internet.[11] He doesn't specify his source for the report (whether, for example, he was personally in touch with Tipton); and he makes no reference to any corroborating testimony from Tipton's friends.

BRIDGE 39 ON THE SHROPSHIRE UNION CANAL

On pages 3 and 15 of his book *Man-Monkey*, Nick Redfern quotes a story from a nineteenth-century source about an experience that allegedly befell the driver of a horse and cart as he was approaching a bridge over the Birmingham and Liverpool Canal (also known as the Shropshire Union Canal) at 10 p.m. on 21 January 1879.[12] A strange black creature, with great white eyes, sprang out of a 'plantation' by the roadside and on to the horse's back.[13] When the man tried to dislodge it with his whip, it went through the entity, and the rider dropped it in fright. The horse broke into a canter. At some point subsequently, the ghostly creature vanished.

Redfern identifies the site of the supposed encounter as what's known as Bridge 39, which crosses the Shropshire Union Canal about a mile to the south-west of the village of Woodseaves in Staffordshire. The road in question is the A519, and the banks of the canal are heavily wooded in that area. Judging from Redfern's research, there may be some truth to the story cited above, because he's obtained first-hand testimony from people who claim to have had strange encounters in the locality. For example, an informant called Bob Carroll related an incident that occurred in the early hours of the morning in what was probably January or February of 1972 or 1973. He was working as a lorry driver at the time and heading for a place where he was due to make a delivery. He slowed down as he approached the bridge and was shocked to see a 'hairy man' storm through the trees and disappear down in the direction of the canal. The figure looked well built, but no more than 5 feet tall. Carroll stopped, turned on his lorry's hazard warning lights, and ran back to where he'd seen the figure. Looking over both sides of the bridge, he couldn't see anything, although he heard what sounded like a baby crying, but a lot louder. When he got back to his lorry, it seemed as if the battery was flat for a minute or two, but then it 'kicked in'.[14]

Another of Redfern's informants, Paul Bell, related having had *two* odd experiences while fishing at the canal, but Redfern doesn't specify precisely how close Bell was to the bridge. On a Saturday afternoon in the hot summer of 1976, he saw a large dark-coloured eel or snake-like creature in the water, moving slowly. Its head resembled that of a black sheep, and was flicking from side to side rapidly. Bell estimated that the creature may have been 10 feet long, if not slightly longer. He had a Polaroid camera with him, but he didn't think to take a snap of it. Therefore, we'll never know whether the experience was objective or hallucinatory.[15] The following Saturday, he was fishing at virtually the same spot when he sensed that he was being watched. Looking across the canal, he was horrified to see a dark hairy face staring at him from thick bushes. It had both human and monkey-like features. But the sighting was very brief, with the creature running into the trees and out of sight. In terms of size, it resembled a large monkey.[16]

Reported sightings of this type haven't been confined to the immediate vicinity of the bridge. For example, a man referred to as Simon informed Redfern about an experience that he'd had in the summer of 1982 while walking beside the canal with a girl-friend. They were about three-quarters of a mile from the bridge.

He saw dozens of birds noisily flying away and heard a sudden loud screaming noise from the other side of the canal. Then he saw a large muscular and agile creature get up and leave. He estimated that its height was, at most, 5½ feet. It looked like a gorilla face-on, but when it turned sideways, Simon noticed that it had a very long muzzle, like a werewolf. His girlfriend was apparently traumatised by the incident.[17]

BRIDGEND, SOUTH WALES

SNAKE PIT WOODS

A UK-based woman who has written under the names 'Steph Young', 'Tessy Rawlins' and 'Stephen Young' is the author of a 675-page book titled *Something in the Woods is Taking People: Five Book Edition*. For this, she has used the pen-name 'Stephen Young'. Confusingly, the main title of this compilation is the same as that of one of the constituent volumes. While much of the book deals with mysterious human disappearances, it has a wider focus. For example, it discusses a spate of apparent suicides, by hanging, among young people in the Bridgend area of South Wales, which began in 2007 with the death of an 18-year-old man called Dale (pp. 309–329).

In respect of these tragic deaths, Young specifically mentions a wooded spot known as the 'Snake Pit' or 'Snake Pit Woods'. But from what I've seen on the internet, I gather that some of the young suicide victims hanged themselves at home rather than in the woods. The fact that multiple people killed themselves in the woods could be because it was a 'convenient' place to commit suicide, or because – for some reason – they wanted to die where others had killed themselves. However, Young views these suicides as mysterious. For example, she refers to a teenager called Jenna Jones, who was found hanging in the woods. A friend of hers, Dan, apparently told reporters that when he'd spoken to her the day before, 'she was completely fine'. And when the mother of Jenna's best friend saw her the night before, Jenna didn't seem to have a care in the world (p. 310).

Young notes that a girl who survived a suicide attempt told a magazine journalist that her head kept telling her to do it, because everything would be all right. After a failed suicide attempt, someone called Justin said that voices in his head had told him to do 'bad things'. He subsequently hanged himself in the woods. However, according to Young, neither of these people had a history of schizophrenia. Leah, another person mentioned by Young, reportedly had no memory of her attempt to hang herself.

Young asks whether something happening in the local area was causing those affected to hear voices, or – worse still – whether the victims were somehow targeted and triggered to commit suicide. She goes on to discuss various conspiracy theory notions, including the suggestion that, as an experiment in mind control and remote influencing, either TETRA (terrestrial trunk radio) towers or telecommunication masts were being used to direct microwaves at a targeted group of young people.

BRISTOL

LEIGH WOODS

Press reports in 2014 related a story about two women who'd abandoned a camping trip after having some disturbing experiences in Leigh Woods, which are near the Clifton Suspension Bridge on the western outskirts of Bristol. According to the *Daily Mail*, the campers were 34-year-old Kate Channon and 28-year-old Lola Swan,[18] although the *Huffington Post* gave Channon's age as 24.[19]

The women erected their tent during daylight. Their hammer went missing during the excursion. As night fell, they began to hear strange noises, and they felt as if they were being watched. At one point, Channon whistled out, and something whistled back. The 'final straw' came at 1 a.m., when they heard a child's voice. Feeling panicky, they packed up their tent and left.

The next day, Swan flicked through some photographs taken the previous night. She noticed an image of what she assumed to have been a ghostly figure watching them. It can be seen in the online *Daily Mail* article. However, to me, it's amorphous, and it seems speculative to attribute it to something paranormal. Similarly, it's unclear whether the noises that the women heard were of a paranormal origin. It's conceivable that they were caused by animals, or by other people (possibly pranksters) who happened to be in the wood that night.

KENT

DERING WOOD, NEAR PLUCKLEY

The village of Pluckley, near Ashford in Kent, has supposedly been the setting for multiple ghostly happenings. It's been dubbed 'England's most haunted village'.[20] Whether the area has seen more than its fair share of truly paranormal events might be questioned. However, in the mid-1990s, in an episode of the television series *Strange but True?*, several witnesses testified to having had ghostly experiences there.[21] For example, a Peggy Theobald reported an occasion when she and her husband had seen a coach and horses, which then disappeared.

One of the supposedly haunted locations in the Pluckley area is Dering Wood, colloquially known as 'Screaming Woods'. It's about a mile and a half west-south-west of Pluckley, and most of it is now owned by the Woodland Trust, which manages it for conservation, small-scale timber production and public access.[22] The main entrance is on the north side of the wood, at the Woodland Trust's car park beside the minor road between Pluckley and Smarden Bell. I visited the wood on a sunny day in October 2018 and found it to be a pleasant spot and not at all creepy. Sadly, though, it seems that the wood's reputation for being haunted may have attracted sensation-seeking people with a lack of respect for the environment.[23]

In a slim book lacking references, a bibliography or an index, Zachery Knowles includes a short chapter on Dering Wood.[24] He mentions a few ghosts that are said to haunt the wood, but he names no witnesses and doesn't give any specific dates for supposed sightings. For example, he refers to an unnamed young man who, at an unspecified date, was walking in the wood and supposedly encountered an apparition of a man hanging from a tree, the figure supposedly being that of an army colonel who'd committed suicide in the eighteenth century.

Knowles states that the bodies of twenty people, eleven of them children, were found in the wood in 1948, and that the corpses displayed no sign of injury or the cause of death. He refers to this as the 'Dering Woods Massacre'. And he adds that local residents had seen lights coming from 'the forest' the night before. (In terms of size, Dering Wood isn't large enough to be considered a forest.) Knowles claims that fifty years to the day after the 'massacre', locals spotted a strange light, shaped like a cobweb, hanging over the woodland for a lengthy time, and that four students disappeared in the wood that night, never to be seen again.

Dering Wood.

Mention of the supposed 'massacre' can be found on YouTube. For example, it's referred to in a video about England's 'most haunted' forests and woods. The video shows what's supposedly a report about it on the front page of a local newspaper, which is dated 2 November 1948,[25] but the alleged newspaper article and the story about the 'massacre' are clearly fabrications. There are fairly obvious give-aways. The price of the paper is shown as '1p'; but decimalisation of the UK's currency didn't occur until 1971. In 1948, there were 240 pence to the pound, and one penny would have been shown then as '1d', not '1p'. The supposed newspaper cover includes a postcode, but they didn't exist in 1948. In the article, there's a photograph of bodies piled on the ground. But the picture was apparently taken in 1945, in Lithuania, not in Dering Wood![26] I strongly suspect that the story about the missing students is also completely bogus. But I don't know whether Zachery Knowles and the maker(s) of the video really believed these tall tales.

WEST SUSSEX

ST LEONARD'S FOREST, NEAR HORSHAM

In 2008, 18-year-old Stephen Foster and 16-year-old Todd Bevis claimed to have had some ghostly experiences while camping overnight near the church of St John the Evangelist at Coolhurst, on the western fringe of St Leonard's Forest. Furthermore, Foster reported a disturbing aftermath. The case received press attention around the time,[27] and eventually featured in an episode of a television series called *Real Horror*. Under the title 'Terror in the Woods', the episode was aired on Channel 4 in early May 2018.[28]

I don't know whether Foster and Bevis's story was a publicity-seeking invention. But in the television episode, screened years after the supposed events, they were still claiming that it was true. They enjoyed making comedy videos. They wanted to do some *Blair Witch*-style filming at a local spooky location. Their alleged experiences during their night in the woods included hearing the screams of a young girl and feeling a strange presence trying to enter their tent. Foster claimed to believe that an evil force had followed him home, because doors had opened and closed by themselves, and he'd seen dark shapes flitting about his bedroom. Following a terrifying night two weeks after the camping trip, he refused to enter his bedroom, and he reportedly took to sleeping on the sofa downstairs. His mother, Caroline, backed up his tale. But over time, the phenomena abated.

CLAPHAM WOOD, NEAR WORTHING

There's a village called Clapham to the north-west of the coastal town of Worthing. Adjacent to it, there's an area of wood-land, known as Clapham Wood. A book titled *The Demonic*

Connection, which was first published in 1987, mentioned UFO sightings in the vicinity.[29] For example, it reported that, in May 1979, a trainee nurse called Leigh Chandler was approaching Clapham on the A259 road around 2.30 a.m. when she saw a glowing orange object, resembling a football cut in half, moving rapidly over the treetops and across the road, going in a southerly direction (p. 21). And the book mentioned other strange happenings in the locality in the 1970s and '80s, such as dogs going missing in the wood. For instance, a normally obedient 2-year-old collie belonging to a local farmer, John Cornford, was last seen heading towards the trees. It failed to respond to calls, and no trace of it was found, despite a thorough search (p. 17). The book also referred to phenomena occurring at Chanctonbury Ring (the site of an ancient hill fort, about 4 miles north-east of Clapham Wood), and at Cissbury Ring (the site of another hill fort, about 2 miles east-north-east of Clapham Wood).

The Demonic Connection suggested that a sinister black magic group had been using Clapham Wood for occult rituals, and it implied that this group was responsible for the deaths of five people (four named, one unnamed), whose bodies were found in the general area between 1972 and 1981. (Only one of the bodies was found in Clapham Wood itself.)

I've presented a detailed examination of the Clapham Wood case in Chapter 6 of my book *Zones of Strangeness*, where I point out that the claims made about this part of West Sussex are controversial, and that there may be normal, non-paranormal, explanations for much of what's been reported. For example, a gamekeeper with a hostile attitude to visiting canines may have been responsible for the dog disappearances in the wood. As for the aforementioned human deaths, *The Demonic Connection* doesn't cite any convincing evidence linking them with the activities of an occult group.

HAMPSHIRE

A PHANTOM LAKE IN THE NEW FOREST

On page 51 of their book *Phenomena*, John Michell and Robert Rickard reproduced a short article from the 10 November 1969 edition of the *Daily Mirror*. It concerned a family who'd reportedly seen a strange sight near Beaulieu Abbey in the New Forest seventeen years previously. John and Christine Swain, and their two sons, were on a minor road when they saw a mist-shrouded lake. About 50 yards from the shore, there was a boulder with a sword stuck in it. They presumed that this was a memorial to the fabled King Arthur. However, despite making some 250 return visits over the years to try to locate the scene again, they'd been unsuccessful.

The newspaper article didn't say whether the family actually stopped their car and got out to view the spectacle. But since it apparently fascinated them, I presume that was the case. However, I've been unable to glean any more information about the incident, and therefore I'm not sure what to make of the report. A possible explanation is that the witnesses experienced an illusion caused by the mist. Some years ago, I was driving east on the A811 road near Buchlyvie in central Scotland when I 'saw' a loch (lake) to my left, in the direction of a low-lying area known as Flanders Moss. This caused a moment of puzzlement, because I was familiar with the road and I knew that there was no loch there. I then realised that it was an illusion produced by an extensive area of ground mist.

There've been other reports of people seeing phantom scenery. Some years ago, a correspondent informed me about a puzzling experience that she and her future husband had had in the summer of 1939. They were in the habit of going for evening walks through the Camperdown Estate near Dundee. On the occasion in question, they entered a clearing in a wooded area and saw a summer house made of logs. There was a paved path leading up to it. The next evening, they went the same way. But much to their dismay, they couldn't find the summer house, and numerous subsequent searches also drew a blank. Perhaps their experience was a shared hallucination. Or maybe their memories were edited by some mysterious process, leaving them with a compelling, but false, recollection of having seen a summer house. If so, did the hallucination or false memory represent a scene that actually existed at some point in the past? We'll doubtless never know.

ACCORDING TO FOLKLORE ...

A number of other woodland locations in Britain are supposedly haunted. However, the reports I've seen about them tend to be little more than vague folklore, since the supposed witnesses go largely unnamed. Accordingly, I shan't discuss them at great length.

MILTONRIGG WOODS, NEAR BRAMPTON, CUMBRIA

At 1.18 p.m. on 30 August 1926, a train passing through Miltonrigg Woods collided with an open motor coach at a level crossing.[30] Seven passengers in the coach died instantly, as did the gate keeper, and another person died shortly after. The ghosts of folklore are typically linked with tragic events, and workers on the railway (now disused) are said to have heard the cries of two young children coming from the site of the collision.

An internet item describes a night-time visit to the wood, in July 2017, by five investigators who were evidently predisposed to think of ghostly manifestations in spiritualistic terms.[31] At one point, as they were driving to a spot close to the scene of the 1926 accident, a member of the team reportedly saw an oncoming train. But by that time, the railway line was no longer in use. At some point after setting up camp, they held a séance, during which one of them spotted a dark shadowy figure wandering on the perimeter of the camp. Later that night, another member of the team saw a similar spectacle – it was around 6 feet tall and translucent. Later, numerous light anomalies were seen soaring through the woodland. Some passed through the camp. Towards 1 a.m., the team began to have problems with their equipment. For example, the batteries of two iPhones, two cameras and a camcorder failed at the same time. But near the end of their visit, they had some response from a 'K2 meter', which is apparently a device intended to pick up energy from supposed 'spirits'.

BRADLEY WOODS, NORTH EAST LINCOLNSHIRE

A wood near the village of Bradley is supposedly haunted by the ghost of a young woman wearing a black cloak and hood. However, the stories about her have a strong 'folklore flavour', and without testimony from named witnesses, one might doubt whether there's much to them.[32]

WOMBWELL WOODS, NEAR BARNSLEY, SOUTH YORKSHIRE

There've allegedly been many reports of ghostly manifestations in Wombwell Woods over the years, although there doesn't seem to be much testimony from named witnesses. The commonest sighting has been that of a male apparition that supposedly resembles Guy Fawkes. It has allegedly jumped out on walkers in the woods. An unnamed couple reported that the figure jumped out at them as they drove past the woods – it covered its face with a cape as they passed through it. Bright balls of light have been reported, and many people have supposedly been attacked in the woods by a force that made them feel so ill that they passed out. We're also told that 'shadow figures' have often been sighted in the area. A paranormal investigator called Phil Sinclair visited the locality and felt that something, claiming to be evil, was mocking him and playing around with his equipment.[33]

HERMIT'S WOOD, NEAR ILKESTON, DERBYSHIRE

Located south-west of Ilkeston, there's a small area of ancient woodland known as Hermit's Wood. People have supposedly heard strange banging noises there, this often being accompanied by their sensing a change from a normal atmosphere to a very oppressive one. Witnesses have allegedly had an overwhelming sensation of being watched and followed. And people have reportedly seen an apparition of a monk or some other hooded form there, the sightings mainly occurring at night. Legend has it that a monk, probably from a local abbey, hanged himself in the wood.[34]

WYCHWOOD FOREST, OXFORDSHIRE

Wychwood Forest is a small area of broadleaf woodland to the south-west of Charlbury. Visitors to the forest have reportedly felt that they were being watched and followed, and also touched by an unseen presence. Many people have supposedly experienced a feeling of nausea, and witnesses have allegedly heard whispers, shouts and sounds of horses in the forest.

A horse-drawn cart, driven by a man, and containing two weeping children, has allegedly been seen there on occasions. A tree in the forest, thought to have been used for hanging criminals, is supposedly a hot spot for activity. People there have allegedly sensed a male presence and experienced feelings of oppression and dread.[35]

In his book *Man-Monkey* (pp. 61–63), Nick Redfern quotes from a magazine article by Jan Williams, who referred to people seeing unusual animals in the area, including a bear or bear-like creature.[36]

PEMBREY FOREST, CARMARTHENSHIRE, WALES

Lying south of Kidwelly, Pembrey Forest is on the South Wales coast and has supposedly been the setting for many strange happenings. Apparitional phenomena have allegedly included sightings of cavaliers, deformed people and Second World War soldiers. Visitors to the forest have reportedly been grabbed around the ankles, to make them fall over; and campers have supposedly found their equipment heaped in a pile, or their cooking implements thrown into the woods.[37]

EPPING FOREST, LONDON/ESSEX

Epping Forest straddles the boundary between north-east London and Essex. Sadly, the present-day forest is much smaller than it used to be. The area has supposedly been the setting for ghostly phenomena, but the reports tend to be of the anonymous folklore type. For example, a newspaper item, available on the internet, refers to Loughton Camp and states that it's thought to have been used as a base by Boudica (a Celtic warrior queen who led an uprising against the Romans in about AD 60), 'and

[that] this has led a number of people to think that the spirits and memories of dead soldiers have been left in the area.'[38] Again, rather vaguely, the article states that a number of accounts have reported muffled sounds of drums and marching coming from the forest, which some people have attributed to the spirits of dead soldiers.

'SALLY IN THE WOOD', NEAR BATH, SOMERSET

A stretch of the A363 road to the east of Bath is known as 'Sally in the Wood', the 'Sally' apparently being the name of a female ghost that has reputedly appeared to motorists driving on the road through this wooded area, which is a few miles north-west of Bradford-on-Avon, Wiltshire.[39] It's supposedly renowned for road traffic collisions, some of which have been fatal.

In April 2008, a number of paranormal investigators visited the area and had some odd subjective experiences, which may have been due to suggestion and imagination rather than anything truly paranormal. Some of the investigators also heard odd sounds.[40] The website item reporting their visit includes an appended account from 'Luke from Bristol', who mentioned a three-day camping trip to the area that he and two elder brothers had made when they were in their early teens. It had been 'amazing' (enjoyable?) during the daytime, but 'tense and uncomfortable at night': what looked like hands pressed into the tent lining; pegs and guy lines were pulled out; and sounds of children (both laughing and crying) were heard coming from outside.

10

REFLECTIONS AND
SPECULATIONS

Although I touched on theoretical ideas in the preceding chapters, my principal focus was on presenting and evaluating case material. In this chapter, I'll mention some intriguing cases from the USA, and then offer some thoughts on what may be behind many paranormal and UFO events.

There are people with an interest in ghosts who don't have much time for the subject of UFOs, and there are people interested in UFOs who seem to know little about the paranormal. And some bigfoot researchers apparently feel uncomfortable about their subject being linked with that of UFOs. But setting aside cases based on misperception, misinterpretation and hoaxes, these supposedly different phenomena appear to be closely linked. Indeed, they may entail the same basic mechanisms and originate from the same source. Certainly, looking back at the cases already mentioned, there does seem to be a lot of overlap. For example, as noted in Chapter 8, visitors to Rendlesham Forest claim to have experienced a wide array of phenomena, and at least two of the witnesses involved in the 'Fife Incident' (Chapter 5) had reportedly experienced ghostly manifestations in addition to phenomena of the UFO type.

Given that there's a degree of interconnectedness between phenomena that have traditionally been considered as belonging to fundamentally different categories, I would urge researchers to ask wide-ranging questions when enquiring about spontaneous paranormal phenomena. For example, when investigating a seemingly 'typical' haunting, it might be worthwhile to enquire whether there've been any 'additional' phenomena, such as UFO manifestations or sightings of strange animal-like entities.

Britain is by no means unique in hosting cases showing the overlap phenomenon. The following are some notable examples from the USA, not necessarily involving woodland. In addition to displaying overlap, they reflect the theatricality that's characteristic of many paranormal events. To me, these cases suggest that there's some sort of intelligence orchestrating the performances.

'OVERLAP CASES' FROM THE USA

FAYETTE COUNTY, PENNSYLVANIA

Stan Gordon's book *Silent Invasion* discusses a rash of UFO sightings and bigfoot encounters that occurred in Pennsylvania in 1972–74. Most of the reports were from the south-western part of the state. A particularly fascinating case came to his attention in the autumn of 1973 (pp. 227–44). The following is a brief summary, and various details have been omitted.

The setting was a rural location outside Uniontown, Fayette County. The events began with a UFO sighting involving a good number of witnesses, including a 22-year-old man whom Gordon refers to as Steve Palmer (pseudonym). Along with two boys, Steve went to a field on his father's farm, where the UFO seemed to have come down. They saw a huge, white domed structure with a flattish base, although previously, when the object was in the sky, witnesses had seen it as spherical and red in colour.

A whirring sound was coming from the UFO, and there was a smell in the air, somewhat like burning rubber. They spotted two creatures coming towards them, which they initially took to be bears. The hair-covered entities had glowing green eyes, no visible neck and long arms. One of them appeared to be over 8 feet tall; the other was about 7 feet in height. Steve fired a tracer shot over them. When he fired a second such shot towards them, the larger creature reached up, as if to grab the projectile, at which point the UFO suddenly vanished, leaving a ring of luminosity where it had been. The whirring sound also ceased. The creatures turned and headed towards a wooded area. Steve fired three live shots at them, but neither creature showed any sign of having been harmed.

Later, Steve returned to the field with an officer from the state police. The luminous ring could still be seen. There was another bigfoot encounter, although from the description in Gordon's book, it seems that it may have entailed only one creature. When Gordon and his colleagues arrived on the scene, later that night, there were further odd occurrences. For example, Steve displayed strange behaviour, one of Gordon's colleagues felt as if he were going to faint, and the air seemed to become permeated with a very strong, sickening smell.

That night appeared to mark a turning point for Steve (now deceased), since he went on to have further paranormal experiences over the years.

YAKAMA INDIAN RESERVATION, WASHINGTON

In his book *Examining the Earthlight Theory*, Greg Long (pp. 56–59) recounts some strange experiences that befell a witness called Jim Miller (pseudonym) one night in December 1975. The setting was the Yakama (or Yakima) Indian Reservation, in the state of Washington.

Driving home on an unlit gravel road, on the northern slopes of the Toppenish Ridge, Jim saw a cow and two calves coming his way. He slowed down. Moments later, he saw three figures at the side of the road. One of them bounded on to the road in a 15-foot slow-motion stride and slowly raised its arms above its head. It was about 7 feet tall.

Feeling uneasy, Jim drove on. The extremely thin and unusually dressed figure had a very long face, a long, pointed nose and very white facial skin. As Jim swerved around the entity, it turned sideways, without moving its arms or changing its expression. Not long after, an elongated, lighted object appeared behind Jim's vehicle, blinking on and off several times. Shortly after that, the inside of the truck and the area immediately around it were brightly illuminated. Jim saw a shadow to his right. Intuitively, he knew that it was the figure of a close friend. He recognised the shape of the latter's head and coat. Speeding on, he heard a woman's voice in his head, telling him to drive recklessly, because 'they' couldn't afford to be the cause of his getting hurt. The ghostly passenger turned to look at Jim, leant forward, and then looked up at the light coming through the windscreen. After leaning back and wiping its eyes, the figure leant forward, as if to get up – and then disappeared. The light vanished, and Jim experienced a feeling that someone had died. The next morning, he learned that a friend, who resembled the figure he'd seen in the truck, had been killed in a shooting incident the previous night. Therefore, as well as seeing humanoids and a UFO, Jim had apparently seen what's known as a *crisis apparition* (i.e. an apparition experienced around the time that the person it represents is undergoing some sort of crisis).

Researchers Bill Vogel and David Akers interviewed Jim. Akers subsequently reported to a colleague that he'd detected nothing to suggest deliberate fabrication or a desire for publicity on Jim's part, although given the night-time conditions and the duration of the incident, he found it hard to account for the amount of descriptive detail. Interestingly, though, Greg Long (p. 58) explains that about three months after Jim's experience, and about 10 miles away, a ranch family saw two tall, white-faced humanoid creatures chasing some of their cattle down a road.

THE 'SKINWALKER RANCH', UTAH

A property that's colloquially known as the 'Skinwalker Ranch' has excited much interest over recent years. It's located about 2½ miles south-west of Fort Duchesne in the north-east of Utah, within an area called the Uinta Basin, which has something of a reputation for UFO sightings and other strange events. The property is said to cover 480 acres (three-quarters of a square mile). It lies within the Uintah and Ouray Indian Reservation, although I gather that the ranch itself isn't classed as tribal land. In the lore of the Native American tribes of the south-western USA, a *skinwalker* is an evil witch who is able to shape-shift into different forms, such as that of a wolf or a bear. During the 1800s, there were tensions between the Ute and Navajo tribes. The Utes apparently came to believe that they'd been cursed by the Navajos. But it's possible, of course, that there's no fundamental connection between the reported phenomena and the area's Native American history and folklore.

SOURCES

The principal sources that I've drawn on are:

- An article by Zack Van Eyck in the 30 June 1996 edition of the *Deseret News*, a Salt Lake City (Utah) newspaper.[1] So far as I know, it was the first publication to draw attention to the alleged phenomena at the ranch. It describes the experiences of a family called Sherman (real name), who bought the property in 1994.

- A book by Colm Kelleher and George Knapp, titled *Hunt for the Skinwalker* (published in 2005).

- A talk given to a conference in 2018 by George Knapp.[2] I'll refer to it as his 'presentation'. It accorded broadly with what's in *Hunt for the Skinwalker*, but there were some discrepancies; and it painted a slightly more dramatic picture. In what follows, I've given much more weight to the book, which was written closer in time to the principal events.

- Chapter 8 of the 2010 edition of a book by Frank Salisbury, titled *The Utah UFO Display*.

- Email correspondence from Frank Salisbury (now deceased).

- Three books by Ryan Skinner, who has reportedly made numerous visits to the area: *Skinwalker Ranch: Path of the Skinwalker* (published in 2013); *Skinwalker Ranch: No Trespassing* (written with a D.L. Wallace, published in 2014); *Skinwalker Ranch: The UFO Farm* (published in 2015). I've reviewed all three of these books in some detail on Amazon. co.uk and Amazon.com.

  - Ryan Skinner's website (www.skinwalkerranch.org).

HISTORY OF THE RANCH

Judging from Frank Salisbury's book, a couple called Kenneth and Edith Myers bought the property around 1933. They started with about 160 acres and subsequently increased their holding by buying further parcels of land. Prior to his death in 2011, Dr Garth Myers, a former paediatric neurologist, informed Salisbury that his brother Kenneth had died in 1987, after which his (Kenneth's) widow had remained at the ranch until about 1992. She died in 1994, whereupon Garth Myers and his sisters inherited the property, which they sold to the Sherman family. (Salisbury describes the family using the pseudonym *Gorman*, which Kelleher and Knapp had used in their book. However, the family's real name, Sherman, is now well known in the public domain, and had, in fact, already appeared in Van Eyck's 1996 article.)

Kelleher and Knapp's book gives a rather different, and somewhat confusing, account of the history of the ranch prior to its acquisition by the Shermans. The authors state that the 'previous owners' (presumably meaning Kenneth and Edith Myers) had bought it in the 1950s (p. 11), and that the property had been unoccupied for almost seven years when the Shermans arrived (p. 8). Admittedly, Van Eyck's (1996) article says something very similar: 'The ranch sat idle for seven years after the previous owners passed away.' Maybe Van Eyck's article was Kelleher and Knapp's source for the seven-year figure. However, given that Garth Myers was a close relative of Kenneth and Edith Myers, I imagine that his version (conveyed to Frank Salisbury) is more likely to be correct.

Robert Bigelow, the property and aerospace entrepreneur, bought the ranch from the Shermans in August 1996. He was financing the Las Vegas-based National Institute for Discovery Science (NIDS), a private research organisation with an interest in anomalous phenomena. It was established in 1995 and became defunct (in name, at least) in 2004. Dr Colm Kelleher, a biochemist by background, was its chief field research scientist from 1996 to 2004. However, his connection with Bigelow and involvement with the ranch didn't permanently end in 2004.

Along with George Knapp (an investigative journalist), Kelleher co-authored the above-mentioned book *Hunt for the Skinwalker*, which mainly focuses on the experiences of the Sherman family and the subsequent investigation, by NIDS, of the ranch and surrounding area. *Hunt for the Skinwalker* isn't an official NIDS publication, although from information given to me by George Knapp some years ago, I gather that the organisation knew of, and didn't object to, the book's publication. So far as I know, Knapp himself was never employed by NIDS. In his 2018 conference presentation, he explained that Bigelow sold the ranch in 2016.

Salisbury's book contains a critical chapter on the case, and while accepting that the ranch has been the setting for genuinely anomalous phenomena, he challenges some of Kelleher and Knapp's assertions.

PHENOMENA PRIOR TO THE SHERMANS' OCCUPANCY

Garth Myers told Frank Salisbury that he'd been close to his brother and sister-in-law, and that nothing strange happened when they were living on the ranch. Salisbury (pp. 220–21) considers the possibility that Kenneth and Edith Myers refrained from telling Garth about UFO experiences because he was sceptical about such matters. But Salisbury indicates that there's only tenuous evidence for that: an associate of Salisbury's, known as Junior Hicks, seemed to recall an assistant at a drugstore telling him that Edith Myers had UFO stories to tell. On the other hand, a rancher called John Garcia, with a property adjoining the Skinwalker Ranch, told Salisbury and Hicks about a UFO sighting that he'd had on his own land when Kenneth Myers' widow was still living at the adjacent ranch. Garcia's wife had seen it, too, but only fleetingly.

Regarding the Shermans' purchase of the ranch, Kelleher and Knapp's book states that the sellers had put some very strange clauses in the property sale contract, stipulating that there was to be no digging on the land without their receiving prior warning. And Kelleher and Knapp state that the Shermans found that every door in the ranch house had several heavy-duty dead bolts on both the inside and outside, that all the windows were bolted and that there were indications that the previous owners had chained large guard dogs to both ends of the building. (Technically, the most recent 'previous owners' would have been Garth Myers and his sisters, but Kelleher and Knapp are no doubt referring to Kenneth and Edith Myers. It would seem that Garth Myers and his sisters owned the property only briefly, and probably never occupied it.) Regarding the matter of digging on the ranch, Garth informed Salisbury that the only stipulation in the real estate contract was one retaining oil rights for the sellers. He denied that there was a profusion of locks at the property, although he told Salisbury that there were small sliding locks on cupboards inside; and he denied that his late brother had ever used large guard dogs. On the other hand, regarding the matter of digging on the ranch, Charles Winn, with a property adjoining the Skinwalker Ranch, told Salisbury that Kenneth Myers was 'very, very fussy about where the ditch company dug a hole or you done any excavation very deep, [because] he said bad things will happen.'

PHENOMENA DURING THE SHERMANS' OCCUPANCY

One of my main sources for this section is Kelleher and Knapp's book. The information it gives about the Shermans' experiences is presumably based on what the family told NIDS personnel or

George Knapp. Terry Sherman was a key witness regarding many of the events mentioned in the book. But it's worth sounding a cautionary note. Salisbury had a number of lengthy telephone conversations with him, and Sherman contended that many of the things in *Hunt for the Skinwalker* only resembled a true accounting of his experiences. He said that he was unaware that a book was being written about his family's experiences, and he said that he'd never met George Knapp, although he'd spoken to him on the phone. However, Sherman was somewhat guarded about what had actually occurred at the ranch. Perhaps there was some sort of non-disclosure agreement associated with the sale of the property to Robert Bigelow in 1996.

Van Eyck's (1996) *Deseret News* article stated that it took a while for the Shermans to remodel the old house and move in. It's worth noting that building renovations sometimes appear to precipitate phenomena of the haunting and poltergeist type. According to Kelleher and Knapp's book, there were indeed such manifestations. For example, doors in the ranch house sometimes opened and closed with great force, and objects would go missing and then turn up somewhere unexpected. According to Van Eyck's article, there was an occasion when Terry Sherman heard male voices, speaking an unfamiliar language. At the time, he was in a field with the family dogs. The source seemed to be about 25 feet above him, but he couldn't see anything to account for the voices. The dogs barked and growled, and then ran off to the house.

According to Van Eyck's article, the Shermans had seen three specific types of UFO repeatedly during the preceding fifteen months: a small box-like craft with a white light, a 40-foot-long object and a 'huge ship the size of several football fields'. And they'd reportedly seen a craft emitting a wavy red ray or light beam as it flew along.

Additionally, according to Van Eyck, the family had seen other airborne lights, some of which had emerged from orange, circular doorways that seemed to appear in mid-air. *Hunt for the Skinwalker* (pp. 62–65) discusses this in more detail, but describes the manifestation somewhat differently. It states that, dozens of times, members of the Sherman family would see 'unworldly orange structures' in the western sky, seemingly hovering low over some cottonwood trees about a mile away. Confusingly, though, *Hunt for the Skinwalker* then switches to the singular, which presumably means that only one such 'structure' was seen on any given occasion. The writer and researcher Christopher O'Brien visited Terry Sherman at the ranch in the summer of 1996, shortly before NIDS acquired the property. According to him, Sherman said that large apertures would open in the air in front of the house, and triangular objects would float through and shoot off smaller objects, which were refrigerator-sized. Sherman mentioned an occasion when one of the objects had struck some cottonwood trees, knocking their tops off. O'Brien saw branches scattered on the ground, but he doesn't say whether the object that had allegedly struck the trees was of the larger or smaller type.[3] Possibly, Sherman didn't specify which type it was. At any rate, the three sources (Van Eyck, Kelleher and Knapp, and O'Brien) describe these events somewhat differently, so we may never know precisely what occurred. Cases of this type tend to be 'messy' when it comes down to the fine details!

Van Eyck's article referred to a flying light that followed Gwen Sherman's car as she drove home from work one night. *Hunt for the Skinwalker* (pp. 52–54) describes what may have been the same incident. But it goes into much more detail. Furthermore, the account is much more dramatic. For example, the UFO is described as a large black, triangular object, not simply a light, as Van Eyck described it.

Hunt for the Skinwalker mentions sightings of orb-shaped objects on the ranch – some blue, some red and some white – but it's not clear from the book whether more than one orb was seen on any given occasion. The book describes an incident that supposedly occurred in April 1996, when three ranch dogs chased after a blue orb that appeared to be intentionally teasing them (pp. 84–86). The dogs followed it into a copse. The next day, Sherman found their incinerated remains in a clearing there, and Salisbury's book (p. 230) notes that Junior Hicks visited the ranch shortly after the incident 'and saw the circles of dead grass with their piles of "grease" in the center.' (Hicks recalled seeing only two circles, but Terry Sherman confirmed to Salisbury that the incident had involved three dogs.) However, Christopher O'Brien (referenced above) questions the date given for the event. He states that he and Terry Sherman were speaking on the phone when the dogs chased after the orb, and he thinks that the incident occurred in the first week of August 1996. On the other hand, in his 2018 conference presentation, George Knapp stated that Sherman had been talking on the phone with Robert Bigelow when the incident began. As I say, when it comes down to details, cases such as this can be messy.

According to Van Eyck's article, at one point, the Shermans discovered three circles of flattened grass in a triangular pattern. They were some 30 feet from one another, and each was about 8 feet in diameter. Other strange soil impressions had been found in a nearby pasture: circles, about 3 feet wide and 1 or 2 feet deep, with the dirt in the middle perfectly flattened.

Van Eyck noted that the Shermans linked the UFO sightings with livestock losses: four of their cows had disappeared without a trace, and three others had been found dead and mutilated. However, on p. 90 of *Hunt for the Skinwalker*, Kelleher and Knapp state that 'someone or something had killed or stolen fourteen registered cattle', which is twice as many as those mentioned by Van Eyck. This discrepancy is puzzling, because the ranch was sold to Robert Bigelow just weeks after Van Eyck's article appeared. It's conceivable, of course, that there was a spate of incidents in those few weeks, although it's also possible that Van Eyck, or Kelleher and Knapp, got the figure wrong, or that the Shermans varied their testimony over time. At any rate, Salisbury's book notes that neighbours also lost cattle. He states that John Garcia had several such stories to tell, including one about a calf found with all of its flesh missing but with no teeth marks on the intact skeleton.

According to *Hunt for the Skinwalker* (pp. 3–9), the Shermans encountered a very large wolf-like creature early in their occupancy. It attacked a calf. Despite being kicked, hit with a baseball bat and then shot several times, it showed no signs of distress and trotted away. Terry Sherman and his son allegedly followed it, eventually losing sight of the creature. But they were able to follow its tracks, until they suddenly stopped, as if the animal had vanished into thin air. However, Terry Sherman told Salisbury that much of this story was based on hearsay, although he wouldn't elaborate. According to Kelleher and Knapp (pp. 26–27), just weeks after the above-mentioned incident, Gwen Sherman had another sighting of a huge wolf-like animal, and – not far from it – was a large black dog-like creature with a disproportionately large head.

Kelleher and Knapp (p. 224) state that the Shermans had often heard sounds of heavy machinery or metallic equipment coming from below the ground.

THE NIDS INVESTIGATION

After the ranch was sold to Robert Bigelow, NIDS employed Terry Sherman to manage it for them. If significant events occurred when NIDS personnel were absent, he could contact the organisation. A private jet was at their disposal, enabling them to fly into Utah and arrive on the scene relatively quickly.

There were competing views within NIDS about how to proceed. One camp argued for 'full instrumentation', with automated sensors covering every square yard of the ranch, constantly feeding back data. Terry Sherman and the other camp thought that that might be counter-productive. In the event, the team opted for a technologically oriented approach, although I doubt whether it went as far as literally monitoring every square yard of the property. In September 1996, a physicist, a veterinarian and Kelleher moved into an observation trailer that had been deployed on the ranch. Over the next few months, they assembled portable equipment for gathering data on UFO lights. Other items available included, for example, night-vision binoculars, video cameras (with night-vision attachments) and radio frequency analysers. Two additional investigators were employed. In the early phase of the project, two teams were deployed on the ranch each night, their task being to capture evidence of anything unusual on videotape or with cameras. And during the early months, dozens of tape-recorded interviews were conducted with local residents concerning strange events that had allegedly occurred near the ranch over the years.

Relatively little was experienced during the early phase of the investigation. *Hunt for the Skinwalker* mentions just two UFO sightings by NIDS personnel (p. 101, p. 105), neither of which seems to have been very dramatic. But there were numerous incidents between March and August 1997. For example, one night in late August, two NIDS colleagues observed an area of yellow light (pp. 143–47). Viewing it with state-of-the-art night-vision binoculars, one of them saw what appeared to be a tunnel suspended a couple of feet above the ground. He saw a black, faceless creature crawl out of it and walk away. His companion, without the night-vision binoculars, saw only an area of yellow light that got brighter and larger and then got smaller and less intense. He took photographs. A very faint, blurry light appeared in one, but there was nothing on the rest of the roll of film.

Incidents also occurred when NIDS personnel were absent. For example, in March 1997, a new-born calf was found mutilated, with its internal organs gone. As in many other animal mutilation cases, there was no sign of blood. In early April 1997, Gwen Sherman made a rare visit to the ranch. She and Terry passed a corral containing four bulls, but forty-five minutes later, they found the corral empty. Shortly after, Terry discovered the bulls, crammed into a trailer, although there was no entrance to it from the corral, except by a tightly locked door. (According to Junior Hicks, as reported by Salisbury, the incident involved a small shed, not a trailer.) NIDS personnel subsequently discovered that something had highly magnetised the metal corral bars near the trailer, although the magnetic field wasn't present on the other side of the corral.

In 1997, NIDS set up six surveillance cameras close to an area on the ranch where a series of dramatic events had occurred, such as the disappearance of six cattle. Some of the cameras could see into the infrared part of the spectrum. The cameras operated around the clock. However, a year passed with nothing unusual being detected. Then, in July 1998, three of them were vandalised in mysterious circumstances.

Terry Sherman had reportedly found that changes made to the topography of the ranch would be followed by UFO sightings. NIDS made attempts to elicit such phenomena by digging on the property. In several instances, within forty-eight hours, neighbours sighted a low-flying orange object that disturbed animals. However, the NIDS personnel themselves didn't see it, and it wasn't detected by their surveillance cameras.

According to *Hunt for the Skinwalker* (pp. 257–58), a perfect circle appeared overnight in February 2002 on the thin ice covering a pond, not far from the ranch house. Examination showed that it had been cut by a sharp object moving anticlockwise. There were ice shavings at the edges of the groove. They were taken for analysis, along with some from a control spot elsewhere on the ice, but the test results showed nothing noteworthy. Magnetic field, electric field and radiation readings were taken in the vicinity of the pond, but Kelleher and Knapp imply that nothing remarkable was found. The cattle were checked for unusual marks, but none were found, and there were no unusual tracks.

As mentioned above, Colm Kelleher is said to have left NIDS in 2004. By then, apart from the discovery of the circle cut into the ice, nothing of note had apparently happened at the ranch for some years.

PHENOMENA SINCE 2004

Ryan Skinner, whose books I've mentioned above, has made numerous investigative trips to the Uinta Basin and has reportedly made clandestine visits to the ranch itself, where he has allegedly experienced some dramatic phenomena. But since I've reviewed his books in some detail on Amazon, I shan't take up too much space by going into detail about them here. Suffice it to say that I've noticed some inconsistencies. For example, his 2013 book and his 2015 book give conflicting accounts of an occasion when a wolf-like creature allegedly materialised near him when he ventured on to the ranch at night. The first book indicates that he was alone at the time. (His brother had travelled to Utah with him but was feeling unwell, and therefore Skinner went on to the ranch by himself.) But according to the 2015 book, Skinner was with another investigator (unnamed) when the wolf materialised (pp. 18–19). He's also inconsistent regarding its size. On p. 18, he describes it as 'massive', but on p. 30, he refers to it as being 'only somewhat larger than average'. I don't know what to make of these inconsistencies. Diehard sceptics could seize on them to disregard all of his testimony. On the other hand, if his primary focus has been on getting out to the area and experiencing as much as he can, it could be that he's had genuinely anomalous experiences, but has been rather careless about note-keeping and accurately describing what he's witnessed.

Skinner's first book claims that after his initial nocturnal visit to the ranch, he experienced haunt-type phenomena for a period in his Wisconsin home. Among other things, Skinner's second (2014) book includes testimony from people who had supposedly worked at the ranch as security guards. Not surprisingly, their real names aren't given. They, too, reportedly experienced unusual phenomena during their time there.

COMMENTS

A hard-line sceptic might dismiss the Skinwalker Ranch case on the grounds that there are different versions of some of the stories and that some of the alleged witnesses are anonymous. However, regarding the general area, there are a fair number of named witnesses, and I think it's unlikely that they all conspired to create a myth about the ranch. Again, from a very sceptical viewpoint, it might be conjectured that the Shermans invented stories about what was happening during their ownership of the property, and that Terry Sherman continued with deception and trickery when he was employed by NIDS as the ranch manager. But I'm not aware of any evidence of that. Furthermore, it's worth recalling that NIDS personnel themselves are said to have witnessed phenomena, including UFO sightings, which would have been difficult, if not impossible, for Terry Sherman to fabricate.

For their part, Kelleher and Knapp (p. 211) think that it's highly unlikely that all of the strange events at the ranch were manufactured by the Shermans. However, it's possible that in some way they catalysed phenomena just waiting to happen. It would be interesting to know whether they'd experienced anything strange *before* they moved to the ranch.

In Chapter 26 of their book, Kelleher and Knapp consider the possibility that highly secret military technology was being tested in the area. They state, rather vaguely, that military personnel were seen in the vicinity on several occasions, and they note, for example, that holographic projections might conceivably account for some of the UFO sightings, and that advanced camouflage experiments could, theoretically, explain some of the other incidents. On balance, though, they think it's unlikely that the ranch was targeted for a covert military operation. They note, for instance, that it's doubtful whether any government on earth had such technology decades ago, when UFO sightings in the Uinta Basin became a matter of public discussion.

In their book *Contagion*, Darren Ritson, and Mike Hallowell suggest that poltergeist activity feeds on fear or stress, and that it may be that 'the polt' deliberately precipitates stress and fear, to enable it to feed (pp. 198–99). They may be right, but it's a strange notion, because fear and stress are mental/physiological *states*, not physical substances or types of energy. However, if we apply their notion to the case of the Skinwalker Ranch, and broaden it, to include more than just poltergeist effects, it helps to make sense of the fact that NIDS personnel seemed to experience fewer dramatic incidents than the Shermans. For the latter, the phenomena were often disruptive and distressing, which may have 'fed' the manifestations. But the NIDS researchers actually wanted paranormal activity to occur, so that they could observe and record it. To the extent that they were less fearful, they may have provided less 'sustenance'. That may be why they were served only tantalising titbits, along with a large dose of frustration.

A RANCH NEAR SEDONA, ARIZONA

In their book *Merging Dimensions*, Tom Dongo and Linda Bradshaw discuss the Sedona area in central Arizona. The first part of the book, by Bradshaw, focuses mainly on a ranch that she and her family had occupied in the area, although she doesn't give its exact location or provide dates for the incidents she describes. The alleged manifestations included, for example, mysterious sounds, unusual lights, photographic anomalies, the malfunctioning of equipment (as a result of unexpected battery drainage) and sightings of unusual creatures. In one such incident, Bradshaw looked out of her kitchen window to see what looked like a silver-grey animal running outside (p. 29). It disappeared before her eyes, and she then realised that it had been 3 or 4 feet off the ground.

In his part of the book, Dongo discusses the area more generally. He suggests that it contains a number of major and minor 'portals' (p. 76). He cites UFO incidents that raise questions about the role of the military. For example, one afternoon in the autumn of 1994, a woman in Village of Oak Creek reportedly saw a jet fighter flying in the company of two silver discs. The latter were about 20 feet in diameter. Several days afterwards, the witness and other residents in the neighbourhood were harassed by two large military helicopters (pp. 113–14).

In her 2012 book *Real Wolfmen*, Linda Godfrey describes some strange experiences that befell a family called Martin at their then home in Palmyra, Maine, in the north-east of the USA (pp. 126–34). However, the family were apparently living in a rural setting, so I presume that their home was actually on the fringe of the town, if not a few miles outside it.

In the UK, at the end of October 2013, the case was featured in an episode of the television series *Paranormal Witness* (broadcast on the Freeview channel Really). Actors helped to recreate the reported events, with interspersed commentary from the principal witnesses. However, there were some differences between this version and Linda Godfrey's portrayal, although they were generally minor. The following outline is based on Godfrey's version. In places, I've noted, within brackets, points where the television version differed from hers, although I haven't sought to comment on all the differences.

About 10.30, one evening in the late summer of 2007, Shelley Martin, then 45, and her husband Eric, then 48, were sitting on their front porch, drinking coffee, when Eric had a 'bad feeling'. He told his wife that she should immediately go back into the house. (But according to the television programme, the year was *2006*, and the incident occurred during the 'Memorial Holiday weekend', which would have been *in late May*.) The couple's two standard poodles (referred to as 'hunting dogs' in the TV programme) had been acting in a particularly nervous manner that evening.

Instead of going back into the house, Shelley 'trained [a] floodlight into the blur of fog'. This revealed three large furry creatures, whose eyes reflected a bright yellow-green colour. They rose and ran on their hind legs. They seemed to be at least 7 feet tall and had short tails and pointed ears. It's not clear from Godfrey's account how long it was before they ran out of sight. But when they did so, Shelley shone her light back on the front yard, seeing two more, which were only 20 feet away, and moving towards her and Eric on all fours. The creatures rose on their hind legs and ran around the house to join the others. The bedroom window of the couple's daughter was on that side of the house, so Shelley and Eric rushed indoors and went upstairs to her room. When they shone the light down to a side yard, the five creatures were seen to be calmly standing on their back legs, staring back at them. The daughter woke up and saw their eyes. But being sleepy, she went back to bed.

The Martins rang the emergency number 911. They were told to call a game warden, who said they should remain in the house and lock the doors. (But according to the television programme, Shelley spoke to someone from the police, and then the call was disconnected.) Shelley and Eric apparently believed that the creatures would have been able to break into the house if they'd really wanted to. Although Eric had some guns, they were locked in the garage (or in a *barn*, according to the television programme). The couple retired to bed around 1 a.m. but had great difficulty in sleeping. Later that morning, it was found that the mysterious creatures had gone. Shelley found what she described as 'over-large dog prints with a "hook" on the end'.

Godfrey explains that weeks before the creatures were sighted, the Martins 'began to see unidentified lights floating near [a] swamp area'. (This wording could be taken to mean that the anomalous lights were seen more than once, but the television programme mentioned only one occasion. It indicated that they were seen from the porch of the house. Shelley stated that the lights were pulsating in some trees. However, when Eric and his son, Sean, went into the woods, to investigate, the lights were no longer visible, and nothing was seen to account for them.) Godfrey refers to two other witnesses, not members of the Martin family, who also saw the lights. (But they weren't mentioned in the television programme.)

Sometime prior to the appearance of the creatures, Eric started seeing an apparition of a little girl in the house. (The television programme didn't mention this.) It seems that on at least one occasion, the sighting was preceded by his hearing footsteps. The haunting apparently continued after the Martins moved out – they learned that an 8-year-old boy, the son of the new tenants, had refused to sleep in his room, because of the 'mean little girl'.

At one point in 2010, Eric happened to be driving past the property when he realised that he'd forgotten his wallet. So he pulled into the driveway, in order to turn around. Although his vehicle had been running well up to then, a ball joint snapped in half and a shaft ripped apart. However, it's conceivable that this breakdown was purely coincidental. (There was no mention of it in the television programme.)

THE BRIDGEWATER TRIANGLE, MASSACHUSETTS

In his book *Mysterious America*, Loren Coleman (pp. 32–39) refers to the Hockomock Swamp region of south-east Massachusetts. It has a reputation for anomalous phenomena and has been dubbed the 'Bridgewater Triangle'. (Towns called Bridgewater and West Bridgewater lie within the area.) Coleman states that the towns of Abington, Freetown and Rehoboth make up the apexes of the triangle, and that it covers about 200 square miles. But as with other alleged hot spots given the label 'triangle', the designation should probably not be taken too literally. Indeed, in an internet article, Christopher Pittman, who's familiar with the area, notes that unexplained phenomena are also common in the towns just outside the triangle.[4]

Coleman (p. 29) explains that 'Hockomock' is the native Algonquian word for the Devil. He equates the Hockomock Swamp area with the Bridgewater Triangle (p. 33). Pittman, however, states that the swamp is the centre of the triangle, which implies that the triangle is larger than the Hockomock Swamp. At any rate, Coleman (p. 34) indicates that the local Indians regarded the Hockomock area as especially sacred, but sometimes evil.

UFO PHENOMENA

Without giving a date, Coleman (p. 35) refers to a report from colonial times of an occasion ('Yellow Day') when the sky over the area shone with an eerie, sulphurous yellow light all day long. He notes that, more recently, there've been many reports of strange lights and noises in the sky over the massive power lines that run through the swamp; and he states that elusive balls of light have been seen every January over the railway lines that run beside Raynham Dog Track and across the swamp.[5]

These manifestations in the vicinity of the power lines and railway lines could, perhaps, be explained in terms of Persinger's tectonic strain theory, which I've discussed briefly in Chapter 3. However, I don't know whether the local geological conditions are conducive to phenomena of the type predicted by that theory.

In his internet article, Pittman states that the first documented UFO sighting in the area occurred on 10 May 1760, in daylight, when a 'sphere of fire' was seen from Bridgewater. However, it was also seen from Roxbury, Massachusetts, which doesn't fall within the Bridgewater Triangle. Furthermore, Pittman implies that the phenomenon was witnessed from elsewhere in New England. Arguably, then, this particular manifestation, whatever its nature, may have been unrelated to the fact that Bridgewater lies within a supposed anomaly hot spot.

Pittman states that there were many UFO sightings in the locality in the mid 1960s, and that reports have continued to come in since then. For example, he relates that five people saw a strange ball of light floating among some trees in Rehoboth in 1968. After they shouted a warning at it, it suddenly expanded to about 5 feet in diameter. It began to move in their direction, and they fled. Pittman relates that a witness reportedly saw a brightly lit craft with numerous red, green and white lights manoeuvring over Assawompsett Pond in Middleboro on 10 December 1998. It split into two objects, which then flew around the sky in geometric patterns, at high speed, exhibiting spectacular coloured lights. The two UFOs then recombined and disappeared. Immediately after the sighting, air force planes were seen over the pond, seemingly searching for something. In recent years, there've been reports of military or military-like helicopters appearing in the triangle, or of helicopter-like sounds being heard there.

Coleman (pp. 35–36) refers to an incident in Rehoboth, in 1973, when a restaurant experienced a short power failure, after which two large circles were found impressed in the dirt behind the building.

MYSTERIOUS ANIMALS

Large, unknown birds have reportedly been seen in the skies over the Bridgewater Triangle, and the area has also been the setting for sightings of bigfoot-type creatures, huge black dogs, big cats and huge snakes. However, although there may have been a good many sightings over the years, the likelihood of any particular person experiencing something odd there may be quite low, at least in respect of bigfoot sightings. In his internet article, Pittman refers to a trapper called John Baker, who had a bigfoot encounter in the area in the early 1980s. But it was the only such experience he'd had in over thirty years of working in the swamp.

On occasions, cattle, sheep, and pigs have been found dead in the area. Coleman (p. 39) relates that in 1976, in Abington, a huge black dog (if that's what it was) ripped the throats out of two ponies belonging to a local fireman, who saw the creature standing over the carcasses, gnawing at their necks. The last sighting of it was by a police officer who fired a shot but seemingly missed, whereupon the mysterious creature turned and slowly walked away.

In his internet article, Pittman notes that the bodies of mutilated animals have been found in Freetown/Fall River State Forest, although the police have apparently attributed this to human agency – to some sort of cult activity. However, Pittman states that no solid evidence of cult involvement has been found.

GHOSTLY EXPERIENCES

'King Philip's War' was an armed conflict in New England in the seventeenth century, between Native Americans on one side and the colonists and their Native American allies on the other. A boulder known as Anawan Rock, located along Route 44 in Rehoboth, was where Anawan, chief of the Wampanoag tribe, surrendered to the colonists. Pittman notes that according to local belief, the spot is haunted by the angry spirits of warriors captured that day, and he cites some experiences that have been reported. For example, a pair of visitors allegedly saw a bonfire blazing on top of the rock. But it then disappeared before their eyes.

Pittman mentions other stories or legends concerning ghostly events in the Bridgewater Triangle. For example, a resident told him that he looked into an old barn window one night and saw a black midget-like form high up on a wall. It seemed to disintegrate and move, like a mist, towards the onlooker, who fled. When he returned later, he saw nothing but heard weird screeching noises.

THE PSYCHIC INTERNET THEORY

Evidence from spontaneous cases and laboratory-based research indicates that some people, at least, have a degree of psychic ability. For example, in poltergeist cases, there's often a 'focal' person, around whom the phenomena occur, and a popular theory is that these people are unwittingly manifesting a 'mind over matter' effect (known as *psychokinesis*). Could it be that many paranormal phenomena are generated by living human beings, and that the effects are sometimes produced, *collectively*, by minds that are able to interact at an unconscious level? Because the latter notion conjures up an image of computers linked to one another via the internet, I'll call it the *psychic internet theory*.

Take, for example, the case of Rendlesham Forest, which has received wide publicity. Could it be that a collective desire to hear of, or personally witness, further phenomena in the forest is actually engendering ongoing manifestations there? The same question can be asked about other sites, such as Cannock Chase. Indeed, we might conjecture that if a spurious case received sufficient publicity, but without people realising that it was bogus, psychic internets could then start to produce real manifestations! Ufologists and psychical researchers might themselves become involved in psychic internets, thereby unwittingly affecting the nature or occurrence of the phenomena under study.

If they exist, psychic internets may function as complex mechanisms rather than as 'higher minds'. If they're able to fabricate evidence of extraterrestrial visitation it might be impossible to tell whether any UFOs have an exotic origin. Similarly, if they're able to fabricate communications from the dead, it might be impossible to obtain incontrovertible evidence of life after death.

Generally, large psychic internets (those with lots of 'members') might be expected to be more powerful than smaller ones. They could persist despite a turnover of 'members'. The analogy of a political party comes to mind: the original founders might leave or die, but with new people joining, the organisation could continue. A more radical possibility is that psychic internets can take on a life of their own, so to speak, and exist independently of any living person, although with the power to draw people in (at a subconscious level) and use them on an *ad hoc* basis.

Of course, if this theory has some validity, it doesn't necessarily mean that *all* genuinely anomalous phenomena are produced in this way. For example, some UFOs could indeed be exotic, intelligently controlled craft from remote places, 'other dimensions' or even from our own future. Arguably, though, the psychic internet theory and the 'higher intelligence theory' (already alluded to and discussed further below) are better able to explain the theatrical quality associated with many paranormal events and UFO sightings, and can more easily account for cases in which multifaceted and recurrent phenomena are associated with particular localities. The two theories aren't burdened by a need to demonstrate something physically unusual about paranormal and UFO hot spots, and they make no recourse to the 'subtle energies' that people of a New Age persuasion talk about. Similarly, they don't require the idea that anomaly hot spots are 'portals' or gateways to other worlds.

PROBLEMS WITH THE THEORY

An immediate problem with this theory is that it ascribes phenomenal psychic powers to the 'unconscious minds' of people. Furthermore, since collaboration and co-ordination are activities that we normally associate with consciousness, the notion that people's minds can interact at a *subconscious* level to orchestrate complex paranormal phenomena is somewhat hard to accept, although some sort of unconscious interaction between people is suggested by reports of telepathic experiences. Another problem is that if the psychic internet theory were true, we might expect there to be many more reports of miraculous healing. For example, in the case of families with very sick children, one would expect psychic internets (formed from the minds of family members and well-wishers) to produce numerous dramatic cures. Sadly, though, there seems to be little or no evidence of that. Therefore, if they exist, there may be severe limits to what psychic internets can do: they may be much better at producing ephemeral phenomena (sightings of ghosts and UFOs, for example) than lasting physical effects of a positive kind.

ORCHESTRATIONS OF A HIGHER INTELLIGENCE

In their book *Hunt for the Skinwalker*, Colm Kelleher and George Knapp state that some members of the NIDS advisory board started to hypothesise that the Skinwalker Ranch was occupied by a 'sentient, precognitive, non-human intelligence' (p. 251). To my mind, the notion that some sort of higher intelligence is behind many UFO and paranormal phenomena rings true. But I'm not convinced that we need to ascribe a geographical or spatial location to it – to say, for example, that it 'occupies' a particular place or comes from, say, a 'parallel universe'. If such an intelligence exists, it may be very much part of our own reality or universe.

From the point of view of the 'higher intelligence' theory, ghostly phenomena and sightings of UFOs or strange creatures can be construed as temporary, dramatic performances. From this perspective, the objects and entities encountered have no independent, continuing existence, and there's no need to assume that they come from 'another place' (a distant planet, another dimension, another time or a parallel reality).

TRICKSTERISH MANIFESTATIONS

In trying to characterise the supposed higher intelligence, one adjective that definitely springs to mind is *tricksterish*. This aspect was very evident in the Skinwalker Ranch case. For example, *Hunt for the Skinwalker* (p. 29) mentions an occasion when Terry Sherman (referred to as 'Tom Gorman' in the book) placed some pliers on a fence post, turned away, and then found them missing when he turned back. And the book reports that the family got used to finding salt in their pepper shaker and vice versa (p. 239).

Christopher O'Brien relates an interesting story from a time when he was living in the San Luis Valley, which runs from south-central Colorado into northern New Mexico.[6] It's been the setting for strange events, such as cattle mutilations and UFO sightings. His experience occurred in 1993, after he'd spoken to members of a family called Sutherland about a bull of theirs that had been found dead and mutilated in June 1980. During the early evening of the day before the bull was found dead, they heard a helicopter flying slowly south over their property. Then, fifteen to twenty minutes later, they heard it again. They saw it rising from the pasture where the dead bull would be found the next morning. It was mustard-yellow, looked old-fashioned and didn't seem to have any markings. It flew back to the north, over their house. Despite extensive enquiries, they were unable to discover where it had come from, but they were told that a helicopter of that type would be extremely rare and would be astronomically expensive to keep in the air. The day after visiting the Sutherlands – i.e. some thirteen years after their seeing the helicopter – O'Brien was at home, reviewing and typing up his interview notes, when he heard, and then saw, a helicopter that matched what the family had seen in 1980. There were other witnesses to this sighting as well. He notes that ever since that experience, he's been absolutely convinced that there's 'a trickster energy, or programme, that is paranormal in nature and [that] somehow this energy/force/entity is manipulating coincidence and manufacturing synchronicity.'

The hypothesised tricksterish higher intelligence might deliberately orchestrate phenomena to tease, bamboozle and cause dissention. If so, it's probably unrealistic to expect UFOs to land on the White House lawn in the full gaze of the media, since that would validate the UFO phenomenon. An 'absurdity factor' might be intentionally built into the orchestrations, perversely ensuring that witness testimony will be doubted or disputed. After all, many people tend to discount *any* stories of paranormal and UFO phenomena, and they might be particularly dismissive of bizarre reports involving manifestations from more than one traditional category. Indeed, bizarre 'overlap' cases may go unreported if witnesses fear that their testimony will be greeted with derision or incredulity.

IS THE INTELLIGENCE MALEVOLENT?

People caught up in paranormal activity often find their experiences perplexing and frightening. The phenomena might even impel them to leave their homes. Poltergeist outbreaks often entail property damage; and cattle and sheep mutilations obviously have financial implications for farmers or ranchers. Take, for instance, a case reported by Dermot Butler and Carl Nally concerning a farm near Feeny in County Londonderry (also known as County Derry), in Northern Ireland.[7] Since the early 1990s, the owners, Gerald and Bridget McLaughlin, have had to endure hundreds of sheep deaths as a result of attacks by an unknown agency that has completely or partially removed the creatures' tongues, and has sometimes inflicted other injuries. As is typical in such cases, the wounds have exhibited clean cuts, as if they'd been carried out with a laser or sharp instrument. In some instances, mutilated sheep were still alive when they were found.

People may suffer long-term ill-health, or even die, as a result of close-encounter UFO experiences.[8] There are reports of pilots disappearing after encountering UFOs. The best-known case is that of Frederick Valentich, who disappeared in a hired Cessna 182 aircraft off the south coast of Australia in 1978.[9,10]

But the story isn't entirely negative. For example, there've been claims of people being cured of cancer by aliens,[11,12] and of bigfoot creatures acting benevolently towards humans (see Chapter 6). If these reports are true, and if the supposed aliens and bigfoots are deemed to be manifestations of a higher intelligence, it would be wrong to describe it as invariably malevolent. But could this 'good-bad duality' be part of a cynical, tricksterish game, aimed at preventing us from gaining a proper understanding of what we're dealing with?

DOES THE TRICKSTERISH INTELLIGENCE FABRICATE MESSAGES FROM THE DEAD?

When spiritualist mediums purport to pass on messages from the dead, they sometimes make surprisingly accurate statements. Sceptics might attribute this to prosaic factors, such as fishing for information and intelligent guesswork. But research suggests that some mediums do indeed acquire information by paranormal means.[13] However, the fact that mediums' statements are sometimes uncannily accurate doesn't necessarily mean that the information has come from the dead.

A frequently raised alternative possibility, known as the 'super-ESP theory' or 'super-psi theory', is that, unwittingly, mediums have tapped into the memories of living people, via telepathy, or have obtained veridical information from elsewhere by extrasensory perception (ESP). However, it isn't clear how such elaborate information-gathering could occur unconsciously. At any rate, the late David Fontana disputed the super-ESP theory, contending that 'we have no laboratory evidence that telepathy, clairvoyance and precognition can produce the amount and quality of information sometimes yielded through mediums.'[14]

Arguably, though, the notion of spirit communication itself amounts to a super-ESP theory, because it implies that the deceased have prodigious ESP powers. Imagine, for instance, that you're at a spiritualist gathering and that a medium relays a message to you from your deceased grandfather, Bill. Now, how does Bill know that you're at the meeting and that there's a medium present? Has he been keeping tabs on you from the other side of the grave? Is he able to scan your diary and email using clairvoyance, to somehow listen in to your conversations, or to read your mind telepathically? Does he even know the content of your sexual fantasies? Or does he follow you about, like an obsessed and shadowy stalker? But that, too, would require ESP, since he would no longer have physical senses. And for Bill to communicate with you via the medium, he would need a telepathic link with the latter. As for Fontana's contention that there's no laboratory evidence that ESP can produce the amount and quality of information that mediums sometimes yield, it may be that formal, laboratory-based studies aren't the most conducive for eliciting ESP, particularly if the subjects are unselected student volunteers rather than people with a track record of exhibiting ESP.

There are cases in which alleged spirit communicators have been unknown to the people present at a séance but have provided verifiable information about the deceased individuals they've claimed to be. They've been referred to as 'drop-in communicators', and in such instances it would appear that the medium hasn't gleaned the information from any of the sitters by telepathy. Furthermore, it's hard to imagine how the medium could have obtained the information by clairvoyance. Indeed, in some drop-in cases, the confirmatory historical information has had to be pieced together from different sources. Fontana refers to the suggestion that coherent information may exist in a cosmic memory bank, but he asserts that there's little evidence to support it.[15] Therefore, at first sight, drop-in cases appear to support Fontana's contention that our consciousness survives bodily death and that spirit communication is a reality. However, another possibility is that a manipulative and deceptive higher intelligence – the trickster – is at work. If so, information known by the trickster about a deceased person (Joe Bloggs, say) might be deliberately fed, telepathically, to a medium. The latter, and his or her sitters, might then be duped into thinking that the spirit of Joe Bloggs is communicating with them.

A series of communications known as the 'cross-correspondences' is often cited as providing some of the best evidence for survival.[16] They spanned about three decades, from 1901, and came through various mediums and automatists. (Automatists are people who produce automatic writing, in which the hand holding a pen or pencil moves of its own volition, and usually without the automatist's knowing what's being written.) And they appeared to be part of a deliberate plan by the deceased communicators (including founder members of the Society for Psychical Research) to provide convincing evidence of their survival. The following (hypothetical) example gives an idea of how the cross-correspondences worked: Mary, an automatist in England, produces some writing referring to a mythical Greek hero. Sally, a medium in the USA, relays a cryptic message. Molly, in Wales, then produces some automatic writing. Researchers then notice that what Molly has written relates to, and makes sense of, the two previous communications.

However, the evidential weight of the cross-correspondences has been challenged. Christopher Moreman reported a study in which correspondences, some quite startling, were found between passages chosen at random from literary works.[17] From the perspective of the trickster theory, it could be argued that the source of the scripts and messages in the cross-correspondences was a deceptive higher intelligence rather than discarnate humans anxious to demonstrate that they'd survived bodily death. Indeed, if we take the trickster notion seriously, the only logical position to take on supposed evidence for survival is an agnostic one.

THE MOTIVES OF THE HIGHER INTELLIGENCE

If there's a unitary trickster intelligence behind a wide array of anomalous phenomena, is it essentially just a resourceful and perpetual prankster, or could it have higher motives? In his book

UFOs & Nukes, Robert Hastings adduces a wealth of testimony linking UFO sightings with the production, testing, storage and deployment of nuclear weapons. There are even reports of nuclear weapon systems malfunctioning when UFOs have been in their vicinity. These reports could indicate that the intelligence behind the manifestations has an interest in the harmful environmental effects, or potentially harmful effects, of human activity, and is perhaps hinting that it could intervene in a big way if we go too far. Alternatively, 'nuke'-related UFO incidents could simply be a matter of the trickster demonstrating that it can operate in any domain of its choosing, including high-security zones.

Christopher O'Brien notes that the livestock sector is one of the most significant contributors to our global environmental problems. For example, 70 per cent of Amazon rainforest that succumbs to slashing and burning is used to expand pasturelands,[18] and he refers to speculation that the mutilation phenomenon is somehow being manifested by the 'collective unconscious', perhaps as a warning to us.[19] I'm not sure whether there is a collective unconscious, and I tend to think of the hypothesised trickster as being a higher intelligence rather than as a part of us. But either way, given the alarming rise in the world's population and the scale of environmental damage caused by humans, it seems that any such message has been very ineffective!

PROBLEMS WITH THE HIGHER INTELLIGENCE THEORY

The theory helps make sense of overlap cases, which are hard, if not impossible, to explain satisfactorily in more traditional terms. However, it's unclear *how* the effects are produced. For example, I've posited that the tricksterish intelligence can induce hallucinations and tamper with people's memories, although I don't know *how* that would be done. But the trickster theory is by no means alone in leaving much unexplained. For example, deeming that 'aliens' are extraterrestrial or 'interdimensional' doesn't, in itself, explain their reported telepathic abilities.

A more serious problem for the theory is that it's hard to see how it could be disproved if it's untrue. Imagine, for example, that the US government disclosed that it had a large collection of crashed spaceships in its possession, and also a large number of preserved corpses, and that these craft and beings were deemed to be of extraterrestrial origin. If the announcement were backed up with testimony from independent specialists, it would obviously lend support to the extraterrestrial hypothesis. However, a dogged defender of the trickster notion could argue that the deceptive higher intelligence had somehow fabricated the items to give a false impression that Earth is being visited by aliens.

Many would argue that if a theory doesn't allow for a definitive test of its truth, it lies outside the domain of science. But it may be that UFO and paranormal manifestations are of a nature that will never fully yield to conventional science. If so, we may be unable to proceed beyond intelligent speculation.

CONCLUDING WORDS

In closing, I'd like to return to the central theme of this book: anomalous events occurring in Britain's woods and forests. I can't say for sure that being in such an environment significantly increases our likelihood of having paranormal experiences. But if it does, it may be related to the effect that a woodland environment has on our state of consciousness. Rob Gandy put this eloquently in his Foreword, where he noted that wooded areas 'have always been places of mystery, sanctuary and enchantment, and are both enticing and unsettling at the same time [and that they] form the backdrop for many of the fairy stories that we are told as children, and are the explicit locations of adventurers such as Robin Hood.'

Speaking personally, I think there's something very special about woods and forests, particularly those of the broadleaf type. I believe that we should be doing more, not only to protect our existing woods and forests, but to expand them, guaranteeing a home for wildlife and ensuring that we, and future generations, don't have to go far to find zones of enchantment.

If readers have had paranormal experiences in our woods or forests, and would like to share them with me, I'd be interested to hear from them. I can be contacted via the History Press.

NOTES

CHAPTER 1 — INTRODUCTION

1. 'The State of the UK's forests, woods and trees', www.woodlandtrust. org.uk/mediafile/100229275/stake-of-uk-forest-report.pdf.

2. If it's pronounced as a word ('you-foe') rather than as three separate letters ('you-eff-oh'), 'UFO' qualifies as an *acronym*.

3. P.A. McCue (2000), 'Haunted work premises', Paranormal Review [a magazine of the Society for Psychical Research], 14, pp. 13–14.

4. Andrew MacKenzie, *Hauntings and Apparitions*, pp. 198–9.

5. David Jacobs, *The Threat*.

6. 'Lyme disease', www.nhs.uk/conditions/lyme-disease.

7. 'Guide to Alabama rot dog disease: How to spot the signs and protect your dog', www.countryfile.com/news/guide-to-alabama-rot-dog-disease-how-to-spot-the-signs-and-protect-your-dog.

CHAPTER 2 — BAD VIBES IN A KENTISH WOOD

1. Phil Chamberlain, 'Verneys', www.spunk.org/texts/pubs/openeye/ sp000938.txt.

2. Excerpt from *Mind Controllers*, www.whale.to/b/victorian_ch_7.htm

3. Robert Irving, 'The Mythologist – The Henry X file', www.mythologist.co.uk/henryxfile.html

4. Kent Messenger Group, *Unexplained Kent*, pp. 47–52.

5. Albert Budden, *Psychic Close Encounters*, pp. 113–18.

6. The OS map of the area renders the name of the wood with an apostrophe (*Short's Wood*). But it also seems to be known as *Shorts Wood*.

7. However, as indicated below, the contention that the engineer detected vibrations is questioned by Justin Williams' testimony.

8. This is the name given in the book *Unexplained Kent*. Verney's booklet and Victorian's book excerpt refer to the person as 'Mr D'.

9. Some of the sources describe the building as being of two storeys but having no windows on the second storey except at each end. But judging from the planning application documents, the building had only *one* storey. It seems that the two upper windows related to the attic.

10. However, as noted, the couple's problems actually began in early September, when there was an increase in noise from the nearby timber yard.

11. The 2015 edition of the 1:25,000 OS Explorer map of the Ashford area (no. 137) mistakenly names Gribble Bridge Lane as 'Cradocks Lane'.

12. We're not told how the car was broken into, or whether the incident was reported to the police.

13. Justin Williams informed me that Verney had provided him with a cassette tape-recording of the noises. Williams commented: 'I cannot remember when the recording was made but it sounded like feedback from a stereo system to me.'

14. Albert Budden (p. 115) also states that Doreen Verney contracted a form of lymphatic leukaemia, but he doesn't specify when or where the supposed diagnosis was made.

15. Electromagnetic radiation is pretty much ubiquitous. After all, ordinary light and radio waves are types of electromagnetic radiation. Therefore, without knowing what sort of radiation was supposedly

detected, it's impossible to know whether it would have posed any danger to the Verneys.

16. Mark Pilkington, 'Humdingers', www.guardian.co.uk/science/2004/jul/22/research.science3.

17. John Dawes, 'The Hum: a legacy from Nikola Tesla', www.bibliotecapleyades.net/scalar_tech/the_hum/index.htm#Contents.

18. R. Douglas Fields, '"Sonic Weapon Attacks" on U.S. embassy don't add up – for anyone', www.scientificamerican.com/article/ldquo-sonic-weapon-attacks-rdquo-on-u-s-embassy-don-rsquo-t-add-up-mdash-for-anyone.

19. Anonymous (2018), 'More sonic attacks?', *Fortean Times*, 370, pp. 26–7.

20. '"Sonic attack" on US embassy in Havana could have been crickets, say scientists', www.theguardian.com/world/2019/jan/06/sonic-attack-on-us-embassy-in-havana-could-have-been-crickets-say-scientists.

21. Justin Williams believes that the engineer was the one from the Maidstone-based firm. As noted above, according to Verney, the engineer confirmed that there were vibrations, as did John Dyus. But Williams' recollection is that he and his colleague were unable to track down Dyus.

CHAPTER 3 — THE GOREBRIDGE LIGHTS

1. Diane King, 'Newbyres Crescent homes demolished years after gas scare', www.edinburghnews.scotsman.com/news/newbyres-crescent-homes-demolished-years-after-gas-scare-1-4048731.

2. 'Deadly gas forces more Gorebridge families from homes', www.midlothianadvertiser.co.uk/news/deadly-gas-forces-more-gorebridge-families-from-homes-1-4354148.

3. Stargate Edinburgh Tours, www.stargateedinburgh.com.

4. See, for example, 'The Gorebridge story', www.jar-magazine.com/in-depth/16-the-gorebridge-story.

5. 'The Dalhousie Castle abduction', scottishandrew.wordpress.com/2009/10/28/the-dalhousie-castle-abduction.

6. Many reports of close-encounter UFO experiences or UFO-related abductions mention the presence of diminutive humanoid beings with a dark grey skin. They're known as *Greys* or *Grays*. Typical features include: heads that are unusually large in proportion to their bodies; no hair; no observable outer ears or noses; only small openings for ears and nostrils; very small mouths; large, slanted, almond-shaped black eyes.

7. Michael Persinger, 'Replies to the most frequent criticisms and questions concerning the tectonic strain hypothesis', www.god-helmet.com/wp/tectonic.htm

8. Longdendale is a valley that extends from the eastern fringe of the Greater Manchester conurbation into Derbyshire.

9. Paul Devereux, 'Earth lights', www.pauldevereux.co.uk.

10. 'The Egryn Lights', inamidst.com/lights/egryn.

11. Paul Devereux, Paul McCartney & Don Robins (1983), 'Bringing UFOs down to earth', *New Scientist*, vol. 99, no. 1373, pp. 627–30. Available at: books.google.co.uk/books?id=k71wgt1p6b0C&pg=PA627&lpg=PA627&dq=Bringing+UFOs+down+to+earth.

12. L.J. Donnelly and J.G. Rees, 'Tectonic and mining induced fault reactivation around Barlaston on the Midlands Microcraton, North Staffordshire, UK', qjegh.lyellcollection.org/content/34/2/195.

CHAPTER 4 — STRANGE SIGHTINGS IN CORNWALL

1. Assuming that this family actually existed, it may be that their names have been changed.

2. 'The Owl Man of Mawnan – A documentary', www.youtube.com/watch?v=y3vmr4o0e5g.

3. Hugo Gye, '"White witches" who conducted "horrifying" ritualistic sex abuse on children as young as three in Cornish coven jailed for 32 years', www.dailymail.co.uk/news/article-2248123.

CHAPTER 5 — THE 'FIFE INCIDENT'

1. Jayess, 'The Falkland Hill incident', jayess.co.uk/index.htm.

2. Marcus Lowth, 'The 1996 Fife UFO incident', www.ufoinsight.com/the-1996-fife-ufo-incident.

3. Malcolm Robinson, 'The Fife UFO (!) incident 1996: "getting to the truth"', available on the Jayess website.

4. According to one of her accounts, 'The Falkland Hill landing: the true story', the UFO experience began as they were *approaching* Newton of Falkland from the west. But judging from another statement from her, 'Testimony of Mary Morrison', it began as they were *leaving* the hamlet on their eastward journey. The latter article can be found on the Jayess website and is also reproduced on pp. 270–73 of Malcolm Robinson's book *UFO Case Files of Scotland (Volume 1)*.

5. By 'main roads', I think Mary was referring to ordinary roads as opposed to 'back lanes' of the type mentioned in respect of Phase 3.

6. Mary's statement 'The Falkland Hill landing: the true story' implies that they approached their parking spot near Newton of Falkland from the east on that occasion. Confusingly, though, it later implies that they'd approached it from the west.

7. Malcolm Robinson reproduces Jane's statement in *UFO Case Files of Scotland (Volume 1)*, pp. 274–77.

8. *Ibid.*, p. 259.

9. *Ibid.*, p. 252.

10. *Ibid.*, p. 258.

11. *Ibid.*, pp. 340–5.

12. Michael Alexander, '"Aliens are among us", claims UFO expert on 20th anniversary of infamous Fife incident', www.thecourier.co.uk/fp/news/local/fife/289564/aliens-among-us-claims-ufo-expert-20th-anniversary-infamous-fife-incident.

13. Tony Dodd, *Alien Investigator*, p. 88.

CHAPTER 6 — CANNOCK CHASE — AN ANOMALY HOT SPOT

1. 'Cannock Chase German Military Cemetery', www.cwgc.org/find-a-cemetery/cemetery/4007266/cannock-chase-german-military-cemetery.

2. David Clarke (2000), 'Spearhead from space?'. In J. Randles, A. Roberts & D. Clarke, *The UFOs That Never Were*, pp. 76–93.

3. Jenny Randles, *Supernatural Pennines*, pp. 203–5.

4. Lee Brickley, *UFOs, Werewolves & the Pig-Man*, pp. 41–7.

5. *Ibid.*, pp. 31–8.

6. Albert BuddeΩn, *Electric UFOs*, pp. 262–8.

7. Thom Powell, *The Locals*, p. 153.

8. *Ibid.*, pp. 145–6.

9. Nick Redfern, *The Monster Book*, p. 206.

10. Nick Redfern, *Man-Monkey*, pp. 39–40.

11. *Ibid.*, pp. 40–1. This incident is also mentioned on pp. 205–6 of Redfern's *The Monster Book*.

12. 'Glacial Boulder – Cannock Chase', www.geograph.org.uk/photo/4030595.

13. Nick Redfern, *The Monster Book*, p. 206.

14. Nick Redfern, *There's Something in the Woods*, pp. 24–5.

15. *Ibid.*, pp. 7–8.

16. *Ibid.*, p. 8. This incident is also mentioned on p. 10 of Redfern's *The Monster Book*. However, the two versions aren't entirely consistent with each other. For example, according to *There's Something in the Woods*, Redfern learned of the incident in June 2006, just days after it had happened, although according to *The Monster Book*, he learned of it in 2007.

17. Lee Brickley, *UFOs, Werewolves & the Pig-Man*, pp. 53–63.

18. 'Big cats on the prowl', www.bbc.co.uk/insideout/westmidlands/series2/big_cats_sightings_puma_panther_west_midlands.shtml.

19. See, for example, Merrily Harpur's book *Mystery Big Cats*.

20. Lee Brickley, *UFOs, Werewolves & the Pig-Man*, pp. 77–88. Brickley's book is inconsistent in how it renders the name of the supposed creature(s), sometimes using a hyphen ('Pig-Man') and sometimes not ('Pig Man').

21. Nick Redfern, *There's Something in the Woods*, pp. 41–2.

22. *Ibid.*, pp. 5–6

23. Nick Redfern, 'Phantom hounds of the woods', theunexplainedmysteries.com/phantom.html

24. The internet link that I previously used to access this article no longer seems to work.

25. Nick Redfern, *The Monster Book*, pp. 366–8.

26. Lee Brickley, *UFOs, Werewolves & the Pig-Man*, pp. 90–6.

27. *Ibid.*, pp. 96–9.

28. Nick Redfern, *The Monster Book*, pp. 206–9.

29. Nick Redfern, *There's Something in the Woods*, pp. 28–30.

CHAPTER 7 — ENCOUNTER IN DECHMONT WOOD

1. The M8 continues west of Glasgow to Langbank, which is about 8 miles east of Greenock on the Clyde coast.

2. Malcolm Robinson, *UFO Case Files of Scotland (Volume 1)*, pp. 141–2.

3. However, Robinson (Vol. 2, p. 257) quotes a statement that Taylor gave the police shortly after his experience. It included the following (the emphasis is mine): 'The top of the object was dome-shaped and had a large flange *around the middle* ....'. Taken literally, this means that the flange *wasn't* at the bottom of the object.

4. Confusingly, though, in the statement that Taylor gave the police (see the previous note), he described the object as being 'about 30 feet high, but not as high as the trees'. That could refer to the height of the object itself or to how far the top of the object was above the ground. If he meant the latter, and if the object itself was about 4m in height, Taylor would have been looking up at the underside of it.

5. Taylor's wife couldn't smell the odour. Campbell doesn't say how long Taylor continued to notice it. He indicates (p. 149) that tests with samples of ozone, nitrogen dioxide and hydrogen sulphide showed that the latter most closely matched what Taylor was, or had been, experiencing, although it wasn't identical. (Campbell doesn't say whether Taylor was still experiencing the aberrant odour around the time the testing was carried out.)

6. Bangour General Hospital was built during the Second World War as an annexe to Bangour Village Hospital for Mental Diseases. It (the general hospital) closed in the early 1990s, and the last wards of the psychiatric facility closed in 2004. The hospital complex was only about half a mile from the site of Bob Taylor's UFO experience. See: 'Bangour General Hospital', archiveshub.jisc.ac.uk/search/archives/e72dd4b8-e70e-38a2-a5bd-aa1181980024.

7. I would have expected the main emphasis to be on a physical examination rather an examination of Taylor's mental state.

8. The assertion that Taylor was 'feeling well' doesn't entirely tally with the report that he continued to experience a feeling of thirst for two days after the incident in the woods.

9. Nigel Watson (1990), 'Livingston – I presume', *Fortean Times*, 56, Winter, pp. 48–9.

10. Phill Fenton, 'The Dechmont Law "UFO" Explained', drive.google.com/file/d/0B8Awe00wVmcQYTNqN2VfM29YQzA/view

11. 'The Dechmont Law UFO', www.amazon.co.uk/Dechmont-Law-UFO-Phill-Fenton-ebook/dp/B0083K5C2K

CHAPTER 8 — RENDLESHAM FOREST

1. Georgina Bruni, *You Can't Tell the People*, p. 27.

2. *Ibid.*, p. 25.

3. *Ibid.*, p. 26.

4. *Ibid.*, p. 28.

5. *Ibid.*, pp. 404–5.

6. *Ibid.*, pp. 367–8.

7. *Ibid.*, pp. 380–1.

8. Nick Redfern, 'The multiple mysteries of Rendlesham Forest', mysteriousuniverse.org/2017/12/the-multiple-mysteries-of-rendlesham-forest.

9. According to subsequent testimony from him, a Staff Sergeant Jim Penniston approached the object and slid one of his hands over its surface, noticing that it felt warm (see pp. 172–86 of Bruni's book).

10. Andrew Pike, *The Rendlesham File*, pp. 659–60.

11. In his interesting book *UFOs & Nukes*, Robert Hastings refers to a claim, by Halt, that beams from one of the UFOs he saw came down in, or near, the weapons storage area (WSA) at the Bentwaters base (p. 409). It's believed that tactical nuclear weapons were kept there. Hastings managed to contact some of the personnel who'd worked in the WSA around that time, but their accounts were rather inconsistent with one another (pp. 413–37).

12. Andrew Pike, *The Rendlesham File*, pp. 522–34.

13. Brenda Butler, Dot Street and Jenny Randles, *Sky Crash*, pp. 347–8.

14. Georgina Bruni, *You Can't Tell the People*, pp. 363–4.

15. *Ibid.*, p. 406.

16. Robert Hastings, *UFOs & Nukes*, pp. 431–2.

17. *Ibid.*, p. 431.

18. Georgina Bruni, *You Can't Tell the People*, p. 379.

19. Alan Gauld & A.D. Cornell, *Poltergeists*, pp. 211–19.

CHAPTER 9 — BRIEFER REPORTS

1. David Clarke, *Supernatural Peak District*, p. 42.

2. A report from the CFZ about the investigation is available on the internet: 'The Hunt for the Bolam "Beast"', www.cfz.org.uk/expeditions/03bolam,

3. Nick Redfern, 'The Ultimate Monstrous Thought-Form?', mysteriousuniverse.org/2018/04/the-ultimate-monstrous-thought-form.

4. *Ibid.*

5. See, also: 'Hell Fire Corner and the Wyke Woods flap', lowercalderlegends.wordpress.com/2010/03/26/hell-fire-corner-and-the-wyke-woods-flap.

6. Jenny Randles, *Supernatural Pennines*, pp. 192–3.

7. 'Solomon's Temple, Buxton', en.wikipedia.org/wiki/Solomon%27s_Temple,_Buxton.

8. Jenny Randles, *The Pennine UFO Mystery*, p. 29.

9. David Clarke & Andy Roberts, *Phantoms of the Sky*, pp. 55–6.

10. Jenny Randles, *The Pennine UFO Mystery*, pp. 33–4.

11. Nick Redfern, 'Horror in the skies', mysteriousuniverse.org/2012/12/horror-in-the-skies.

12. G.F. Jackson (edited by C.S. Burne), *Shropshire Folk-Lore*, pp. 106–7.

13. Literally, a 'plantation' is an area of artificially planted trees, not a patch of natural woodland. I don't know whether that's what the writer meant.

14. Nick Redfern, *Man-Monkey*, pp. 87–8.

15. *Ibid.*, pp. 92–3.

16. *Ibid.*, p. 95.

17. *Ibid.*, pp. 57–9.

18. Richard Spillett, 'The real Blair Witch project', www.dailymail.co.uk/news/article-2628099/Terrified-campers-fled-woods-hearing-chilling-voice-child-1am-capturing-ghost-like-vision-camera.html.

19. 'Blair Witch "ghost" terrorises woodland campers in Bristol', www.huffingtonpost.co.uk/2014/05/14/blair-witch-ghost-terrorises-woodland-campers-bristol-pictures_n_5324125.html.

20. Hugh Morris, 'Is Pluckley still England's most haunted village?', www.telegraph.co.uk/travel/destinations/europe/united-kingdom/england/kent/articles/pluckley-still-the-most-haunted-village-in-england.

21. *Strange but true encounters – Pluckley* (ITV, 1995), www.youtube.com/watch?v=5MAg5iA_jCc.

22. 'Dering Wood', www.pluckley.net/village-life/village-amenities/dering-woods.

23. Patrick Sawer, 'Ghost hunters accused of damaging ancient woodland featured on TV', www.telegraph.co.uk/news/2017/10/04/ghost-hunters-accused-damaging-ancient-woodland-featured-tv.

24. Zachery Knowles, *Real Haunted Woods and Forests*, pp. 42–6.

25. '5 most haunted forests & woods In England', www.youtube.com/watch?v=Q8-4dKrtTSA.

26. Dave Godden, 'The Screaming Woods', www.ghostconnections.com/The%20Screaming%20Woods.htm.

27. 'Horsham teenager's poltergeist fears', www.wscountytimes.co.uk/news/horsham-teenager-s-poltergeist-fears-1-826915.

28. George Harrison, 'A murderous doctor, a tortured girl and an abandoned plague pit: The terrifying camping trip behind tonight's True Horror', www.thesun.co.uk/news/6192820/true-horror-camping-doomsday-church.

29. Toyne Newton is the only author named on the cover of the first (1987) edition of *The Demonic Connection*, although the title page refers to 'Toyne Newton *with* Charles Walker & Alan Brown' (my emphasis). However, all three names appear on both the cover and the title page of the 1993 edition, without the word 'with' linking Newton's name with the others. Presumably, then, Walker and Brown are to be regarded as co-authors of the 1993 edition, although the text (which implies that there's only one author) hasn't been updated. The 1987 edition is in hardback, whereas the 1993 edition is a paperback. The only other difference is that the latter contains fewer photographs than the first edition.

30. 'Report on the accident at Naworth Station level crossing on 30th August 1926', www.railwaysarchive.co.uk/docsummary.php?docID=2333.

31. Warren Rome, 'Miltonrigg Woods—a truly haunted place', medium.com/@Authorofthemacabre/miltonrigg-woods-a-truly-haunted-place-e245a745bd9d.

32. 'The Black Lady at Bradley Woods', www.lincolnshireinfo.co.uk/north-east-lincolnshire/bradley/black-lady-bradley-woods.

33. 'Haunted convicts tunnel, Wombwell Woods, Barnsley, UK', paranormalhauntings.blog/2018/05/10/haunted-convicts-tunnel-wombwell-woods-barnsley-uk.

34. 'Hermit's Wood - Derbyshire, England', www.ilkestontown.co.uk/hauntedplaces/hermitscave.html.

35. Helen Murphy Howell, '"If you go down to the woods today..." Britain's Haunted forests', hubpages.com/religion-philosophy/If-You-Go-Down-To-The-Woods-Today-Britains-Haunted-Forests.

36. Jan Williams (1994), 'If you go down to the woods today', *Animals & Men*, July issue. (Page range not specified by N. Redfern, who cited this reference.)

37. 'Pembrey Woods', www.hauntedhovel.com/pembreywoods.html.

38. Joseph Flaig, 'Epping Forest's haunted history', www.guardian-series.co.uk/news/localhistory/11689188.epping-forests-haunted-history.

39. Judging from a Google map, the name 'Sally in the Wood' also applies to a stretch of minor road that branches north off the A363. See: www.google.com/maps/@51.375597,-2.2901975,15z.

40. Maria Williams, 'Sally in the Woods', www.twilightshadowsparanormal.co.uk/sallyinthewoods.html.

CHAPTER 10 — REFLECTIONS AND SPECULATIONS

1. Zack Van Eyck, 'Frequent fliers?', www.deseretnews.com/article/498676/FREQUENT-FLIERS.html?pg=all.

2. 'Skinwalker Ranch: presentation by George Knapp with Q&A', www.youtube.com/watch?v=sg8iK2OGVLE.

3. 'High strangeness at Skinwalker Ranch with Chris O'Brien', www.youtube.com/watch?v=ioMYuJ8OWX4.

4. Christopher Pittman, 'The "Bridgewater Triangle"', www.cellarwalls.com/ufo/btriangle.htm.

5. Coleman's book was first published in 1983. I don't know whether this phenomenon has been witnessed every January since then.

6. Christopher O'Brien, *Stalking the Tricksters*, pp. 70–3.

7. Dermot Butler & Carl Nally, *Circle of Deceit*.

8. See, for example, the late Bob Pratt's book *UFO Danger Zone: Terror and Death in Brazil – Where Next?*.

9. Richard Haines, *Melbourne Episode: Case Study of a Missing Pilot*.

10. Richard Haines & Paul Norman (2000), 'Valentich disappearance: New evidence and a new conclusion'. *Journal of Scientific Exploration*, vol. 14, no 1, pp. 19–33.

11. Christopher O'Brien, *Secrets of the Mysterious Valley*, pp. 97–8.

12. P.A. McCue, *Zones of Strangeness*, pp. 452–7.

13. See, for example, the late David Fontana's book, *Is There an Afterlife?*

14. *Ibid.*, pp. 103–14.

15. *Ibid.*, pp. 113–14; p. 157.

16. *Ibid.*, pp. 175–85.

17. C.M. Moreman, 'A re-examination of the possibility of chance coincidence as an alternative explanation for mediumistic communication in the cross-correspondences', *Journal of the Society for Psychical Research*, vol. 67.4, 2003, pp. 225–42.

18. Christopher O'Brien, *Secrets of the Mysterious Valley*, p. 415.

19. *Ibid.*, p. 426.

BIBLIOGRAPHY

Anonymous. (2018). 'More sonic attacks?'. *Fortean Times*, 370, pp. 26–27.

Brickley, L. (2013). *UFOs, Werewolves & the Pig-Man: Exposing England's Strangest Location – Cannock Chase*. Yam Yam Books.

Bruni, G. (2001). *You Can't Tell the People: The Cover-up of Britain's Roswell*. London: Pan Books.

Budden, A. (1998). *Electric UFOs: Fireballs, Electromagnetics and Abnormal States*. London: Blandford.

Budden, A. (1999). *Psychic Close Encounters*. London: Blandford.

Butler, B., Street, D. & Randles, J. (1986). *Sky Crash*. London: Grafton Books. (First published by Neville Spearman in 1984.)

Butler, D. & Nally, C. (2018). *Circle of Deceit: A Terrifying Alien Agenda in Ireland and Beyond*. Flying Disk Press.

Campbell, S. (1994). *The UFO Mystery Solved: An Examination of UFO Reports and their Explanation*. Edinburgh: Explicit Books.

Clarke, D. (2000). *Supernatural Peak District*. London: Robert Hale.

Clarke, D. (2000). 'Spearhead from space?'. In J. Randles, A. Roberts & D. Clarke, *The UFOs That Never Were*. London: London House. pp. 76–93.

Clarke, D. & Roberts, A. (1990). *Phantoms of the Sky: UFOs – A Modern Myth?* London: Robert Hale.

Clelland, M. (2016). *The Messengers: Owls, Synchronicity and the UFO Abductee*. Rochester, New York: Richard Dolan Press.

Coleman, L. (2007). *Mysterious America*. New York: Paraview Pocket Books.

Devereux, P. (with Clarke, D., Roberts, A. and McCartney, P.) (1990). *Earth Lights Revelation: UFOs and Mystery Lightform Phenomena – The Earth's Secret Energy Force*. London: Blandford.

Devereux, P., McCartney, P. & Robins, D. (1983). 'Bringing UFOs down to earth'. *New Scientist*, vol. 99, no 1373, 1 September, pp. 627–30.

Dodd, T. (1999). *Alien Investigator: The Case Files of Britain's Leading UFO Detective* London: Headline, London.

Dongo, T. & Bradshaw, L. (1995). *Merging Dimensions: The Opening Portals of Sedona*. Sedona, Arizona: Hummingbird Publishing.

Downes, J. (2006). *The Owlman and Others*. Woolfardisworthy, Bideford, N. Devon: CFZ Press.

Fontana, D. (2006). *Is There an Afterlife?* Ropley, Hants.: O Books.

Gauld, A. & Cornell, A.D. (1979). *Poltergeists*. London: Routledge & Kegan Paul.

Godfrey, L. S. (2012). *Real Wolfmen: True Encounters in Modern America*. New York: Tarcher/Penguin.

Gordon, S. (2010). *Silent Invasion: The Pennsylvania UFO-Bigfoot Casebook* (edited by R. Marsh). Privately published.

Haines, R.F. (1987). *Melbourne Episode: Case Study of a Missing Pilot*. Los Altos, California: L.D.A. Press.

Haines, R.F. & Norman, P. (2000). 'Valentich disappearance: New evidence and a new conclusion'. *Journal of Scientific Exploration*, vol. 14, no 1, pp. 19–33.

Halliday, R. (1998). *UFO Scotland*. Edinburgh: B&W Publishing.

Harpur, M. (2006). *Mystery Big Cats*. Wymeswold, Loughborough: Heart of Albion Press.

Hastings, R. (2017). *UFOs & Nukes: Extraordinary Encounters at Nuclear Weapons Sites*. (2nd edition). Privately published.

Hennessey, A. (ed. by Charles, S.R.) (2017). *Alien Encounters and the Paranormal: The Scottish Experience*. Privately published.

Jackson, G.F. (ed. by Burne, C.S.) (1883). *Shropshire Folk-Lore: A Sheaf of Gleanings*. London: Trübner & Co.

Jacobs, D.M. (1999). *The Threat: Revealing the Secret Alien Agenda*. New York: Fireside.

Kelleher, C.A. & Knapp, G. (2005). *Hunt for the Skinwalker: Science Confronts the Unexplained at a Remote Ranch in Utah*. New York: Paraview Pocket Books.

Kent Messenger Group (2011). *Unexplained Kent*. Derby: Derby Book Publishing Co.

Knowles, Z. (2017). *Real Haunted Woods and Forests*. Published by True Ghost Stories.

Long, G. (1990). *Examining the Earthlight Theory: The Yakima UFO Microcosm*. Chicago: J. Allen Hynek Center for UFO Studies.

McCue, P.A. (2000). 'Haunted work premises'. *Paranormal Review* [a magazine of the Society for Psychical Research], 14, pp. 13–14.

McCue, P.A. (2012). *Zones of Strangeness: An Examination of Paranormal and UFO Hot Spots*. Bloomington, Indiana: AuthorHouse.

MacKenzie, A. (1982). *Hauntings and Apparitions*. London: Heinemann.

Michell, J. & Rickard, R.J.M. (1977). *Phenomena: A Book of Wonders*. London: Thames & Hudson.

Moreman , C.M. (2003). 'A re-examination of the possibility of chance coincidence as an alternative explanation for mediumistic communication in the cross-correspondences', *Journal of the Society for Psychical Research*, vol. 67.4, pp. 225–42.

Newton, T. (with Walker, C. and Brown, A.) (1987). *The Demonic Connection: An Investigation into Satanism and the International Black Magic Conspiracy*. Poole: Blandford.

Newton, T., Walker, C. & Brown, A. (1993). *The Demonic Connection: An Investigation into Satanism and the International Black Magic Conspiracy*. Worthing: Badgers Books.

O'Brien, C. (2007). *Secrets of the Mysterious Valley*. Kempton, Illinois: Adventures Unlimited Press.

O'Brien, C. (2009). *Stalking the Tricksters: Shapeshifters, Skinwalkers, Dark Adepts and 2012*. Kempton, Illinois: Adventures Unlimited Press.

Pike, A. (2017). *The Rendlesham File: Britain's Roswell?* (2nd edition). Flying Disk Press.

Powell, T. (2003). *The Locals: A Contemporary Investigation of the Bigfoot/Sasquatch Phenomenon*. Surrey, British Columbia: Hancock House Publishers.

Pratt, B. (1996). *UFO Danger Zone: Terror and Death in Brazil – Where Next?* Madison, Wisconsin: Horus House Press.

Randles, J. (1983). *The Pennine UFO Mystery*. St Albans: Granada.

Randles, J. (2002). *Supernatural Pennines*. London: Robert Hale.

Redfern, N. (2007). *Man-Monkey: In Search of the British Bigfoot*. Woolfardisworthy, Bideford, N. Devon: CFZ Press.

Redfern, N. (2008). *There's Something in the Woods: A Transatlantic Hunt for Monsters and the Mysterious*. San Antonio, Texas: Anomalist Books.

Redfern, N. (2017). *The Monster Book: Creatures, Beasts and Fiends of Nature*. Detroit, Michigan: Visible Ink Press.

Ritson, D.W. & Hallowell, M.J. (2014). *Contagion: In the Shadow of the South Shields Poltergeist*. Limbury, Luton: The Limbury Press.

Robinson, M. (2017). *UFO Case Files of Scotland (Volume 1): Amazing Real Life Alien Encounters*. Privately published.

Robinson, M. (2017). *UFO Case Files of Scotland (Volume 2): The Sightings, 1970s – 1990s*. Privately published.

Salisbury, F.B. (2010). *The Utah UFO Display: A Scientist Brings Reason and Logic to Over 400 UFO Sightings in Utah's Uintah Basin* (2nd edition). Springville, Utah: Bonneville Books.

Skinner, R. (2013). *Skinwalker Ranch: Path of the Skinwalker*. Lulu.

Skinner, R. (with Wallace, D.L.) (2014). *Skinwalker Ranch: No Trespassing*. Privately published.

Skinner, R. (2015). *Skinwalker Ranch: The UFO Farm*. Voodoo Creations LLC.

Victorian, A. (1999). *Mind Controllers*. Frog Ltd.

Watson, N. (1990). 'Livingston – I presume'. *Fortean Times*, 56, Winter, pp. 48–9.

Williams, J. (1994). 'If you go down to the woods today'. *Animals & Men*, July issue. (Page range not specified by N. Redfern, who cited this reference.)

Young, S. (2014). *Something in the Woods is Taking People: Five Book Edition*. Privately published.

INDEX

The History Press

The destination for history
www.thehistorypress.co.uk